The Scrapbooking Journey

A Hands-On Guide to Spiritual Discovery

Cory Richardson-Lauve

Foreword by Stacy Julian, founding editor, *Simple Scrapbooks*

Walking Together, Finding the Way®
SKYLIGHT PATHS®
PUBLISHING
Woodstock, Vermont

The Scrapbooking Journey:
A Hands-On Guide to Spiritual Discovery

2007 First Printing
© 2007 by Cory Richardson-Lauve

The author is grateful for the contributions from other scrapbookers, both in the "Voice along the Journey" pieces and in the reproductions of scrapbook pages. Reprinted by permission.

The names and situations of the teenage girls mentioned in this book have been changed to maintain their anonymity.

Library of Congress Cataloging-in-Publication Data
Richardson-Lauve, Cory.
The scrapbooking journey : a hands-on guide to spiritual discovery / Cory Richardson-Lauve, foreword by Stacy Julian.
    p. cm.
Includes bibliographical references.
ISBN-13: 978-1-59473-216-4 (quality pbk.)
ISBN-10: 1-59473-216-7 (quality pbk.)
1. Photograph albums. 2. Scrapbooks. 3. Spirituality. I. Title.

TR501.R53 2007
745.593—dc22

2007001580

10   9   8   7   6   5   4   3   2   1
Manufactured in the United States of America
Cover Design: Jenny Buono

SkyLight Paths Publishing is creating a place where people of different spiritual traditions come together for challenge and inspiration, a place where we can help each other understand the mystery that lies at the heart of our existence.

SkyLight Paths sees both believers and seekers as a community that increasingly transcends traditional boundaries of religion and denomination—people wanting to learn from each other, *walking together, finding the way.*

SkyLight Paths, "Walking Together, Finding the Way" and colophon are trademarks of LongHill Partners, Inc., registered in the U.S. Patent and Trademark Office.

Walking Together, Finding the Way®
Published by SkyLight Paths Publishing
A Division of LongHill Partners, Inc.
Sunset Farm Offices, Route 4, P.O. Box 237
Woodstock, VT 05091
Tel: (802) 457-4000   Fax: (802) 457-4004
www.skylightpaths.com

To the young people in our care—
past, present, and future—
and to all others seeking peace.
May they find solace in the journey.

Contents

Foreword

Scrapbooking started out for me as just something fun to do—a creative outlet. I loved being able to play with paper and paste while preserving hoards of pictures at the same time. In the beginning I was fascinated by the artistic nature of scrapbooking, the colorful bits and pieces that I could use in designing pages. As I became experienced, the potential to share my stories and to write intrigued me more. Then one day—I'm not sure exactly when it happened—I realized that I didn't love scrapbooking so much for the cute pages or the personal expression as I did for the way it was shaping me. Scrapbooking is making me a better person. I'm more aware of beauty in everyday life, more conscious of change in people around me, and more grateful for my own perspective. Because of scrapbooking, I am better able to recognize and relish fleeting moments that become priceless memories.

Cory Richardson-Lauve says it this way:

> *There is something deep within scrapbooking that fulfills us even beyond our artistic sensibilities. It stirs something in the soul. When I scrapbook, I feel empowered and connected and hopeful. I feel grateful and content and stimulated. In the process of scrapbooking, I feel the closest to my essential self, and to God.*

I've been involved with the scrapbooking industry from its inception. I've read countless articles and books, and I can honestly say that Cory has captured better than anyone I know the culmination of my feelings about scrapbooking. In *The Scrapbooking Journey*, Cory asks the right questions so that you can discover your personal answers. Her words, if you allow them, can enlarge your understanding of the potential you have to improve your life through this amazing hobby.

Thank you, Cory.

Stacy Julian
Founding Editor, *Simple Scrapbooks*
Founder, Big Picture Scrapbooking

Introduction

Meditative. Healing. Communal. These are not words you would easily partner with a hobby that has sparked a three-billion-dollar industry. But there is so much more to this craft than acid-free paper and repositionable adhesive. Scrapbooking is a way of preserving family stories and legacies that goes far beyond a photograph album.

While a photograph album holds pictures, a scrapbook attaches meaning to them. It expands the images to tell who, what, when, and where. Scrapbooks also reveal something about the creator of the page. Why did she take that picture? Why are these images important to her? How do they make her feel?

Scrapbook pages are personal works of art—art infused with the vision, photography, and words of the scrapbooker. The term "artist" may make you uncomfortable; it was difficult for me at first, too. Although I've always loved art of all types—dance, music, painting, sculpture, theater, poetry—I never saw myself as an artist. I thought of artists as free, unconventional people who were different from me. I was in the other category: pragmatic, conventional, secure, even boring at times. But the more scrapbooking has captivated me, the more I've realized that art flows in and around all of us. I've found art and artists surrounding me—and within me. We are all artists.

But there is something deep within scrapbooking that fulfills us even beyond our artistic sensibilities. It stirs something in the soul. When I scrapbook, I feel empowered and connected and hopeful. I feel grateful and content and stimulated. In the process of scrapbooking, I feel the closest to my essential self, and to God.

My Scrapbooking Journey

I started scrapbooking when I was a teenager. I would take the "scraps" of my life—photographs, ticket stubs, prom napkins, and colorful titles ripped from *Teen Magazine*—and combine them into pages that were simple and fun. After I got married, I started exploring new ways to enhance my pages. I used lots of cardstock, stencils, decorative scissors, and fancy corner rounders. I had not yet learned about design concepts; I just loved arranging paper and photographs. It made me happy. So for a few years I made simple pages on my own. Then, on a crisp fall day, I read my first scrapbooking magazine. Artwork poured out of it. Women told the stories of their lives through photographs and words, and I was captivated by the colors, the designs, the textures, and the connections.

My love for scrapbooking grew and is evident in almost every part of my life today. I see "photographs" everywhere, even when I don't have my camera. I notice patterns and wonder how they might combine into pages. I experience moments as gifts that can be captured, if not on paper, then in my heart.

My husband, John, and I work as Teaching-Parents with troubled teenage girls. I cannot imagine a fuller life. It teaches me to celebrate. It teaches me to let go. It teaches me to love. But because my life can get loud and complicated, I've come to love scrapbooking as a quiet and solitary pursuit. My scrapbook journal pages, especially, tend to be eclectic in style—I am constantly exploring new ways to visually represent my musings. You won't find unity in my pages! Some are graphic, some are artsy. Some have muted colors and some are bright. But each page combines images, thoughts, and feelings that express a brief insight or reflection from a moment in time.

Keeping a Scrapbook Journal

I have written this book in the context of my own journey, but I hope the book will come to be about your journey, too. Whether you are a beginning scrapbooker or an experienced, published designer and artist—or anything in between—as long as you are a seeker, there is a place for you in *The Scrapbooking Journey*. I see this book as a dialogue—a conversation between you and me, between you and yourself, and between you and God. Not just a place to read and observe, but a place to participate and grow.

That is why I encourage you to take the time to ponder and answer the questions in this book in a journal.

I've always loved questions—both asking them and being asked. I think it is the questions in our lives that help us define who we are, where we've been, and where we are going. Questions open us up to ourselves and to others. They free us from the need for certainty because they invite more questions. One of my favorite quotations speaks truthfully about questions:

> *I would like to beg of you, dear friend, as well as I can, to have patience with everything that remains unsolved in your heart. Try to love the questions themselves, like locked rooms and like books written in a foreign language. Do not now look for the answers. They cannot now be given to you because you could not live them. It is a question of experiencing everything. At present you need to live the question. Perhaps you will gradually, without even noticing it, find yourself experiencing the answer, some distant day.[1]*

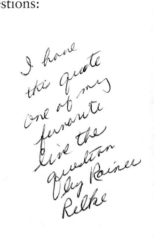

I have this quote as one of my favorite live the question by Rainer Rilke

Questions help us grow; they keep us unstuck. Every day, our lives pose questions:

> *How do you see the world?*
>
> *What is important to you?*
>
> *How do you incorporate what you value into your daily life?*
>
> *Are there things you want to let go of?*
>
> *Are there new ways you want to grow?*

Scrapbooking is a way to make our answers tangible and visible, to discover new facets of ourselves. I think that is why the process of scrapbooking resonates so deeply with people across the world. It gratifies our search for truth and identity. And the scrapbook journal in particular takes the focus off the events of our lives and places it, instead, on the person behind the creating.

Journey and journal have the same root word. They are both from Old French, with the root *journ*, meaning "day." Both journeys and journals mark the passing of days. How appropriate that they go hand in hand: a journey to live and a journal in which to keep a record of living. The journey is about the process: what and who and how you see along the way. So, too, is the journal about the process: how you create and why you create and who you are while you are creating.

Each chapter of *The Scrapbooking Journey* concludes with a "scrapbook journal" experience that invites your active consideration and participation. Scrapbook journal pages are different from typical scrapbook pages in that they are more private and more experimental. They are a place to explore, to answer questions, to pose more questions. They are a place to play and try new things, a place separate from the habits of the past or the accolades of the future. I hope you will give yourself permission to fully participate in these scrapbook journal experiences as you read this book.

Things You'll Need

Trimmers, cutting mat with craft knife, and sharply pointed scissors.

Gluestick, glue dots, double-sided photo tabs, dimensional foam dots, and sticker-maker.

In addition to a blank journal, there are some basic things you will need for the scrapbooking experiences suggested in this book:

Sheets of cardstock or a book
You choose the size: 12 x 12 inches if you prefer a spacious landscape, 6 x 6 inches or 5 x 7 inches if you like to keep things tiny and private. Shop for something that suits you. Or, if you prefer, start with just cardstock. Use a dimension that will slip easily into an album in the future (6 x 6, 8 x 8, 8½ x 11, or 12 x 12 inches). Make sure you have enough pages for the eight scrapbooking journal experiences in the book (either single pages or double-page spreads).

Images
A scrapbook page does not have to focus on a photograph or an image, but it is a good

place to start. Consider using photographs (taken by you or someone else) or other images that represent the pieces of your life, such as ticket stubs, drawings, brochures, programs, or clothing tags.

Stickers, brads, flowers, rub-ons, and other scrapbooking supplies.

Scrapbooking supplies

You will need a paper trimmer for cutting straight lines and scissors for cutting shapes and ribbons. You may also find that a cutting knife and mat will help you with more intricate shapes.

You will also need some kind of adhesive, such as photo tabs made for scrapbooking, a glue stick, or double-sided tape. I like to use an adhesive that is repositionable, so I can easily rearrange the elements on my page.

Acrylic and foam stamps.

Other supplies depend on your budget and can range from simple pens to a set of paints, a variety of rubber or acrylic stamps, inks, a sewing machine, magazine clippings, scrapbooking products (such as rub-ons, stickers, ribbons, patterned papers, and cardstock), and a computer. (See Appendix A for ideas on scrapbooking supplies and techniques.)

A variety of stamping inks.

In the end, *The Scrapbooking Journey* is not about scrapbooks; it is about the *process* of scrapbooking. Finding ourselves as creators can change many aspects of our lives, from little things— such as the clothes we wear and the decorations and furnishings in our homes—to big things—such as the way we spend our free time and the way we see the world. Opening up to other scrapbooking artists can teach us humility and hopefulness and create a sense of community. Telling our stories through scrapbooks today helps make us better people for tomorrow. Creating art grounds us and opens us to our Creator.

Welcome to the journey!

A Voice along the Journey

KAREN RUSSELL

I used to think scrapbooking was silly. But that was before I became a scrapbooker.

From the world outside, looking in, I'm sure we scrapbookers *do* look a little silly with our excitement over the newest patterned papers, our chatty online forums, and our never-ending quest for the perfect adhesive.

But, as an insider, I have to say that *I* think we scrapbookers might just have a slight edge on the rest of the world. A slight edge because we "get it"—the bigger picture. What really matters in life. And maybe we "get it" because we are sitting in front of a 12 x 12-inch (or an 8½ x 11-inch) piece of cardstock on a regular basis, asking ourselves, *What do I really want to remember about my life? What's really important to me?* Maybe, because we are examining our priorities and documenting our memories with a glue stick in hand, defining with photos and paint and chipboard and metal embellishments what we value most.

It really is a beautiful thing.

And as lucky as our families will consider themselves one day to inherit our truckloads of strap-hinged albums, that's not *really* why we do it—that's just a bonus.

We do it for ourselves. We do it for that quiet time late at night while the rest of the world is sleeping. In our pajamas, listening to a little music, surrounded by a clutter of stickers and scissors and photos and ribbon. Completely immersed in the process. Completely content.

We're moms and wives and housekeepers and employees. We're students and cooks and chauffeurs and nose-wipers. We're dreamers and planners and daughters and teachers. We're artists.

And so we *need* those quiet hours to ourselves every now and then.

And we can even take a little "razzing" from the outside world about scrapbooking: the *Saturday Night Live* parodies, the slight snicker that we sometimes get when we bring up the word *scrapbooking*, the notion that what we do isn't anything more than gluing a few photos to a piece of paper.

Because *we know* it's so much more.

1

*R*esonance
Finding Your Focal Point

The first rule of focus is this:
"Wherever you are, be there."

—UNKNOWN AUTHOR

What resonates with you?
What moves you deeply?
What makes you ache, listen, cry, scream, love?

Maybe it is a memory of a moment.
Maybe it is a photograph.
Maybe it is a quotation.
Maybe it is a song lyric or a piece of handmade paper.

Whatever it is, it can become the focal point of a scrapbook page. Ultimately, a scrapbook is a home for all the things that resonate within us, that awaken us with their meaning and depth. A scrapbook is a place to hold the events and moments that beg us to remember them. Scrapbooking captures gifts of time. It impels us to clear out the clutter and focus on the things that really matter.

A Window into Your Life

For where your treasure is,
there your heart will be also.

—MATTHEW 6:21 (NRSV)

If I asked you to name the focal point of your life, you might think "my children" or "my husband" or "my aging mother" or "my dog, Rufus." But what I really want to know is *what*, not *who*. What is the focus of your energy? When you are being a mother, is it all about nurturing? Or teaching? Or learning? Or feeling connected emotionally? All of these, perhaps, but if you look closely, you will find one thread that connects the important elements in your life. Why do you have the friends you have? Why do you nurture the relationships in your life? Why do you go or not go to a place of worship? Why do you have your particular hobbies and interests?

The focal point of my life is learning. For a while, I thought it was teaching, but after a few years I became restless. I was teaching better than ever, but I had stopped learning. It was time for me to learn something new. I longed to be challenged in new ways. This pattern runs throughout my life. Although I spend a lot of time teaching, it is, for me, a conduit to my focal point—learning.

To find our focal point means to search for purpose and meaning, and to live with that intention. In fact, I would go so far as to say this is our mission in life: to find our focal point, our essence. The rest—whether that is what swirls in our closets or refrigerators or in our minds—is secondary.

My friend Susan talks about the clutter in her life. Her house is full in a magnificent way—with pieces of her life and her children's activities scattered throughout. Paper and magazines occupy every flat space. Cooking supplies and recipes hug the counter between meals. Projects wait patiently for her return. Books beg to be read. And she has this marvelous capacity to work within it all; a lap or a corner of a table is all she needs. But she tells me that if she could get to the bare bones of what moves her and motivates her, she would be set free in some ways. She talks about the projects swirling in her mind. She talks about her hopes for organization and focus. She longs to declutter.

For all of us, the challenge comes in deciding where to focus our time, energy, and priorities—and what needs to be ignored or put aside in order to do this. That's where scrapbooking becomes a metaphor for life: Each time we create a page, we have thousands of choices of colors, textures, and designs. Each decision becomes a microcosm that reflects what we value.

Scrapbooking also requires that we decide what *not* to use. We don't need or want every color on one page. We must choose certain photographs and reserve others for later projects. As we focus on a topic and select items that enhance it, each scrapbook page becomes a small window into our lives, a picture of what we value.

As I created a recent page about a childhood visit to Washington, D.C., with my grandfather, I started with two photographs of him and me. One, slightly blurry, shows me straddling his shoulders, both of us laughing. The second was shot from behind as we walked together toward the display of Christmas trees. They are simple candid photos, preserving my

seven-year-old fashion choices and his surprisingly unlined face. But the real treasure in the pictures is what they say about our interactions, what they communicate about our relationship. They reveal our easy companionship and playful joy as we walked and laughed together. So simple, but so significant. You can tell I trust him, that he is my playmate and caregiver. We look so comfortable together.

My grandfather and I don't see each other very often

anymore, but when I look at these pictures, I know part of him is still with me all the time. I am overwhelmed with gratefulness for these images of our time together, and more importantly, for the relationship they illustrate. Whenever I laugh, whenever I trust, whenever I look forward with optimism, it is because of early childhood experiences such as this. I love being able to preserve a moment like this on a page, to celebrate the gifts of family.

What gifts await you on your scrapbook pages? Each page has the potential to return you to your focal point. A strange thing happens in scrapbooking. You may be looking through a narrow lens at your past, but your mind broadens those images into the fullness of life. The past becomes alive again, and you become aware: aware of yourself as a creator, aware of what matters to you, aware of profound connections, aware of the deeper meaning of your life.

A New Sense of Time

*It is when you are really living in the present—work-
ing, thinking, lost, absorbed in something you care
about very much—that you are living spiritually.*

—BARBARA UELAND

It is easy to conclude that someone who spends a lot of time scrapbooking lives in the past. A scrapbooker is consumed with images and stories that are not happening right now, but that happened yesterday or last year.

The paradox is that scrapbooking is not about the past. It is about using the past as a tool to fully experience the present. It is a way of allowing time to be still. By taking the time to remember, we live each moment. And we become more aware.

Time is a human construction, as I am always reminded when we change our clocks in the spring and the fall, or when I call my friend Ben who lives in California. Humans have created a system of keeping time for our convenience, so we can coordinate schedules and talk about "when." Clocks and calendars make us aware of this artificial passing of time—so aware, in fact, that time becomes the fundamental architect of the structure of our days.

And we do have a sense of chronology. Things happen in a particular order; we remember the past and look forward to the future. This moment today is different from a moment tomorrow. We see people grow and seasons change.

But there is another sense of time that the Greeks called *kairos*. Madeleine L'Engle describes it beautifully in *Glimpses of Grace*:

> *Kairos. Real time. God's time. That time which breaks through chronos with a shock of joy, that time we do not recognize when we are experiencing it, but only afterwards, because kairos has nothing to do with chronological time. In kairos we are completely unselfconscious, and yet paradoxically far more real than we can ever be when we are constantly checking our watches for chronological time. The saint in contemplation, lost (discovered) to self in the mind of God is in kairos. The artist at work is in kairos. The child at play, totally thrown outside himself in the game, be it building a sand castle or making a daisy chain, is in kairos. In kairos we become what we are called to be as human beings, co-creators with God, touching on the wonder of creation.[1]*

The creative pursuit of scrapbooking can make us more aware of this expansive way of experiencing time. Scrapbooking can lead us to kairos time.

In a way, scrapbooking is similar to meditation: it quiets the mind. The clock no longer matters. When I scrapbook, I lose sight of insignificant things. I forget about how I look. I'm no longer self-conscious. The appearance of my house doesn't matter. The messy bathroom is ignored. Trivial things disappear. Unfinished conversations and overdue obligations and fleeting emotions are gone. For just a little while, I become aware of only what matters in this moment: the placement of paper and image, this expression of my truth.

Scrapbooking puts me in touch with time on a larger scale. When I look through the pages of my scrapbooks, I see the movement of my life, the beauty of all its seasons, the faces of dear companions. The pages illustrate my faith: a holy awareness of truth and beauty and all that is good.

On my shelf of scrapbooks is a large album that I created about the eighteen months my husband, John, and I spent working at Boys Town in Omaha, Nebraska. It was a time of intense learning and growth, and poignant memories. It was an adventure for John and me that drew us away from our families and closer to each other. I remember the concepts we learned there well, but it is difficult to recall the details of that year and a half.

Except that I have preserved them. As I flip through the pages of my *Blessings of Boys Town* scrapbook, I am transported. I am once again planting flowers outside our home in the rich Midwest soil. I am washing dishes at our sink that overlooked a small goat pasture. I am walking through the cornfields mid-morning after successfully getting our four boys off to school.

And I am feeling the struggles and triumphs of working with troubled teenage boys, adjusting to a working partnership with John, and slowly building deep relationships with our neighbors. And then, I'm escaping to the sites of our vacations: the Grand

Tetons, New Orleans, and Vermont, where we reunited with our loved ones.

It would be so easy to have only a hazy memory of this special time in my life and our marriage. But because I gave myself over to the creative process three years ago, I have a treasure for a lifetime—a treasure that reminds me of the gifts of time. Time is fluid. If we let ourselves, we can flow through the past, present, and future, and find ways they connect. This Boys Town scrapbook from the past propels me to the present and the future. It encourages me to ask: What gifts am I finding in my life today? What moments are hidden blessings? What am I learning? How am I celebrating? What do I want to preserve to revisit in three, ten, or thirty years?

This is the way of scrapbooking. When you scrapbook, and when you look at scrapbooks of your past, you find that you are living in a moment that connects you to a larger sense of time, a clearer glimpse of what is important. Even if it seems that your focus is merely on photographs, paper, and words, in the big-picture sense, you are connecting with your memories, with your own creativity, and, most important, with the Source of all that is—past, present, and future.

A Renewed Clarity

And sometimes, I allow myself to imagine that
each moment in which we love well by simply being
all of who we are and being fully present allows
us to give back something essential to the
Sacred Mystery that sustains all life.

—ORIAH MOUNTAIN DREAMER, *THE INVITATION*

My husband, John, and I work and live with troubled teenage girls as Teaching-Parents. We live in a caring, structured, family-style community, teaching social and independent skills. It is not just a job—it is a lifestyle. Most of the time, I adore this lifestyle. There's so much energy and joy in eight teenage girls! Working with them is rewarding. But some days are rough. Sometimes the rules and structure and caring are too much for a particular girl, and she rebels by being as nasty and unlikable as possible. She will glare disdainfully, slam doors, or yell obscenities.

At first I despair. I start thinking that I'll quit tomorrow and go work at a coffee shop, where there can't possibly be stress or hardship like the harsh rejection I receive from people I'm trying to love. But then I remember why I am here: I want to learn. That is my focal point. I long to be closer to God through greater knowledge, to strengthen my sense of God's presence within me.

And, last time I checked, these things don't come easy. They have to be learned over a lifetime of struggles and disappointments and breakthroughs. So, with a sigh, I find my center once again. I remember and reframe my experience. Those nasty glares can teach me compassion. That shrieking voice can teach me to let go. Her refusal to follow instructions reminds me that, when it comes down to it, I have no control over some aspects of my life.

On those hard days, when my life becomes a prayer and a lesson, I use scrapbooking to help me regain my focus, to get reconnected with what is important. Scrapbooking induces me to accept the lessons and stillness and craziness of life, and it brings me full circle back to what is essential. It reminds me of my mother's advice to "always keep your necklaces clasped, even when you're not wearing them." She taught me that the secret to avoiding tangles was to keep each necklace connected in an unending circle.

Life's knots are all too familiar: stress, fatigue, irritability, tension, anger, too much to do, too little time, too many demands. But if we can stay connected to what is important, we can keep from getting tangled in the knots.

John and I have been married for eight and a half years, and we work together every day. You can imagine the tangles of our relationship and the occasional irritability, frustrations, and problems with communication. One day I'll forget to tell him about the conversation I had with a teacher or caseworker. The next day he'll forget to complete the paperwork for a meeting. Marriage is difficult. Working together is difficult. We don't need photographs to document that.

But I am so grateful for the photographs that document our joys together. During the past year I made a scrapbook page with photos that our friend Jonathan took of the two of us. John and I are sitting on a bench—laughing, touching, snuggling. We are so familiar with each other. My hand is on his face. He tries to kiss me while I playfully pull away. We gaze at the camera, arms around each other. I kiss him on the forehead. Our partnership, illustrated in these photographs, is safe, silly, and easy. It is real and comfortable. Even though it is not perfect, it is beautiful.

Beauty and hope and miracles … sometimes they slip away or get lost in our memories or in the day-to-day busy-ness of life. The gift of scrapbooks is that they hold these gifts for us on the days that our lives do not.

The Gift of the Journey

Be happy for this moment. This moment is your life.

—OMAR KHAYYAM

In October, John and I went on a paddling journey on the Nantahala River in the Smoky Mountains. It had been years since

I'd approached the water, not for any particular reason except that I'd found so many other ways to spend my time, such as scrapbooking and taking photographs. The prospect of getting wet and (probably) cold and even possibly muddy did not excite me as a way to spend my time. But this was a special trip to an exceptional river, and I was excited to revisit my summer-camp days.

I always forget how metaphorical a journey can be. Floating down the Nantahala, I had the sense that I was no longer just in a boat, but in my life. Like a careful, spirited friend, the river carried me. I was moving to a destination, most likely, but I realized that if I focused on "getting there"—wherever "there" was—I would miss the many twists and turns, the beauty and adventures along the way.

I think that is why scrapbooking is so good for me. Instead of focusing on the end result, I can get lost—beautifully lost— along the way. If I'm not too careful or too analytical or too self-critical of what I'm doing, I can become immersed in the process of remembering and re-creating. Memories become feelings, and feelings become treasures to be savored. When I let go and enjoy the process of creating, the destination (the finished page) is no longer the goal. The true gift is the journey.

When I first started scrapbooking, I shunned most scrapbooking supplies. My favorite supplies were my paper cutter and neutral-colored cardstock. Patterns, textures, and shapes had no place on my pages. I was cautious. I tried to maintain an understated color scheme throughout my scrapbook. I carefully controlled the elements on each page and did not let the content (photographs and memories) dictate the form. There was no sense of flow or experimentation.

Slowly, though, my pages started to come alive. After a few trips to a nearby scrapbooking store, I began to experiment with patterns, colors, and texture. Orange and turquoise and violet added energy. Beads and fibers and buttons added texture and interest. Mostly, they helped me embark on the journey of creating, in allowing colors and textures to sing, happy in the exploration and discovery of the moment.

The journey metaphor reminds us to make the *moment* the focal point, to be fully present. To listen to the joy and grief in the moment. To find the gift and the lesson in the moment. Scrapbooking allows us to honor each moment, which in turn makes our life journey rich and meaningful.

A FOCUSING EXPERIENCE

Project: To create a scrapbook journal page identifying the focal point in your life.

If you've lost focus, just sit down and be still. Take the idea and rock it to and fro. Keep some of it and throw some away, and it will renew itself. You need do no more.

—CLARISSA PINKOLA ESTES

NOTE: This is the first of eight scrapbook journal projects in this book. Each is designed to help you explore and grow in your spiritual life. Before you start, make sure you've read the "Things You'll Need" section of the Introduction. This provides the basic outline of what you need to get started. Then set aside a time when you can give yourself to this experience. Keep in mind that scrapbook journal pages are different from typical scrapbook pages. They are more private and more experimental. They are a place to explore, to answer questions, to pose more questions. They are a place to play and try new things.

1. Start by writing your responses to these questions:

What motivates you?

What sustains you?

What would an observer of your life say matters the most to you?

Try to respond in terms of a concept or an idea, not a person. Make a list of your responses. If people's names come to mind, write them down, then probe deeper.

> *What is it about these relationships that keeps you focused on them?*
>
> *What do you do in these relationships that you enjoy or find satisfying?*
>
> *How do you find your truest self in the context of these relationships?*

Use verbs as much as possible in your responses. Words such as learn, pray, nurture, create, teach, lead, care, enjoy, defend, make peace, play, unite, communicate, love, protect, laugh, survive, and connect will help you identify your focus more clearly.

2. Look at your responses. Circle the word that best describes the focal point at this time in your life. There are probably several options, but narrow it down to one word to focus on for this scrapbook journal page.

3. Stop and think about your word for a few minutes. Take a few minutes to respond to each question.

> *What are the ways you live out this word?*
>
> *How does it show up in your life?*
>
> *What relationships help you with it?*
>
> *How do other people experience this aspect of you?*

4. Now choose one or more photographs or pictures that convey this word. (The photographs can be of other people, as long as they illustrate your word.)

As you select your image, consider the *meaning* of the photo or picture. Don't just pick the most engaging picture. For example, if you are creating a page about a birthday party, and you have ten pictures from the event, ask yourself some questions. What was meaningful to you about the party? Was it the joy in the face of the guest of honor? The number of candles on the cake? The strength of the community who attended the party? The beauty of the homemade cake? The variety of gifts that were received? Pick one of these themes that spoke to you during the party and choose your pictures accordingly.

Likewise, for this exercise, consider pictures that illustrate the verb you have chosen as your focal point. Don't just use a self-portrait; try to find pictures of you living out this verb. Take some new photographs if you need to!

5. Consider other elements you might want to add to your page: a title, a drawing, a quotation, some words from your journaling. Such supportive details can create balance and movement. (We'll do more with this in chapters 2 and 3.)

6. Consider which mediums you want to use to create your page: paint, paper, stitching, stamps, markers, stickers, digital technology. As you become more experienced as a scrapbooker, you will find that certain supplies and techniques speak to you—both in general and on specific pages. There are many supplies available. Be open, but be selective. You don't need them all.

1-1

This leads me to insert a word of advice. I can't write about scrapbooking without writing about shopping. Scrapbooking is a very product-driven hobby; manufacturers clamor for our attention and money. The industry is vibrant and growing, and it feeds on scrapbookers' love of texture, shapes, and color. When I walk into a scrapbook store, I experience the same thing that happens when I walk into a home-design or supply store. Although I enter the store perfectly happy with my possessions, not lacking anything

1-2

1-3

except for some light-bulbs (hence the trip to the store) … WHAM! Suddenly, I need every-thing. I need that pair of scented candles, three matching picture frames, a beaded table runner, and two magazines.

When I walk through the door of my local scrapbook store, I immediately see at least three new, cheerful lines of papers that beg for my attention. Maybe some textured letters to accompany them, or some cute swirly rub-ons, or something—anything—with beads or glitter. Ahh … I am in a heaven of possibilities, surrounded by the creativity of other women.

My advice? Enjoy your trips to the scrapbook store. Purchase what you love. But remember that it's okay not to have it all. The amount of your creativity is not linked to the size of your supply collection. Don't allow the shopping to eclipse what scrapbooking is really about. There's a creative force in you that will find its own expression … with whatever materials you use.

1-4

7. Okay, now you're ready to get to the heart of this exercise: how will you emphasize your focal point? Here are some helpful techniques for creating a strong focus on the page:

- *Use contrast. Place a light focal point on a dark background. Or place a light border around a dark focal point. Lighter tones will draw the eye to that element. (See layout 1-1.)*

- *Use repetition. Repeating an image or a word will highlight its importance. Note the repetition of the word love on the background of layout 1-2.*

- *Use size. Enlarge the focal point. Or create a larger border around it to distinguish it from the others. Note the prominence of my mom's face against the backdrop of smaller photographs of flowers on layout 1-3.*

- *Use line. Draw attention to your focal point with horizontal or vertical lines that lead the eye toward it. You can use lines of text (such as titles), arrows, linear doodles, stripes, lines of the edges of other elements, or lines within photographs. Note how the dark line of circles on layout 1-4 draws attention to the word Mom in the title and ends at the most recent picture of her, which ties in with the journaling.*

1-5

- *Use shape. A circle will stand out among right angles. A square will stand out among natural, flowing shapes. (See layout 1-5.)*

- *Use texture. Adding three-dimensional elements (such as flowers, sequins, or ribbons) around the focal point will draw the eye. On layout 1-6, I added a white paper flower to the lower left of the title and a rhinestone and glittery circle above the title.*

- *Use a frame. Even a two-sided frame will help delineate the focal point. (See layout 1-7.)*

- *Use color. Color is a powerful way to direct the eye. (We will explore more of this in chapter 6.)*

1-6

8. Once you have some ideas in your mind, you may want to draw a quick sketch of your page. It is not necessary to plan all the details, just to start with an intentional idea. You can add other embellishments or supporting images as you work. Creating is a process, and you might be surprised by what appears on the journey. Be open to ideas as they come. Even when you start with a rough plan, your page will evolve as you work.

9. As you work, keep returning to your main idea: the focal point. Make sure that you are emphasizing this idea throughout your design.

10. Continue working until you feel your page communicates your thoughts and feelings and visually pleases you.

11. Then take some time to reflect on your page.

Which elements did you spend the most time creating?

What does the page tell you?

What is most meaningful to you about the page?

Are you satisfied with your focal point?

12. Show your page to friends or family members. Look at their eyes.

1-7

Where do they look first?

What draws their attention?

Is it what you had intended?

What does their response tell you?

13. Give yourself some reflection time.

Are you happy that this is the focal point of your life?

If yes, how can you emphasize this focal point throughout your life?

If no, what do you want to change?

If you'd like to see how Heather Preckel and I interpreted this focal point exercise, see "To Learn" and "Nurture" on the color insert.

Going Deeper

Options to explore your focal point further.

> *Either you look at the universe as a very poor cre-*
> *ation out of which no one can make anything, or*
> *you look at your own life and your own part in the*
> *universe as infinitely rich, full of inexhaustible inter-*
> *est, opening out into the infinite further possibilities*
> *for study and contemplation and interest and praise.*
> *Beyond all and in all is God.*
>
> —THOMAS MERTON

✳ Create a scrapbook page with a song or poem as a focal point. Pick words that are meaningful to you. Try to get the entire page to emphasize your message. Place your lyrics or poetry in a meaningful spot on the page and help draw attention there with design techniques and images.

✳ Create a scrapbook page depicting your day and your feelings about the way you spend your time. Start by keeping an activity journal of your day. How *do* you spend your time? Are you doing what really matters to you? Are you aware of a focal point?

✳ Create a scrapbook page showing what the focal point of your life was when you were a child (ten years old or so). Use photographs of you or other images that resonate.

✳ Create a scrapbook page depicting what you want to be caring about ten years from now.

✳ Draw a sketch for a scrapbook page that illustrates the focal points in your life. Size the photos according to your emotional and spiritual investment in each subject. Now, sketch another layout about those focal points. This time, size the photos according to the amount of time you spend on them. Are the sketches similar? Vastly different? Which page do you want to create?

✳ Scrapbook a page about a recent day in your life. What was the focal point of that day? What resonated with you? How you can illustrate these gifts with photos and words?

Notes ———

A Voice along the Journey

KATJA KROMANN

Scrapbooking is both huge and small in my life. It is small in that creating a layout only takes about a couple of hours or so, making it an excellent medium to allow me to play without major commitments or consequences. It is huge in that it expresses who I am in the world. It is a creative outlet that connects me deeply with my spirituality, with something much bigger than myself—something universal, divine.

I sometimes use prompts during the creative process. A favorite prompt of mine is: What if this were the exact opposite? How can I push the boundaries of this idea? This will usually give my idea an unexpected twist and turn.

In the critical moment of inspiration—when the key ingredients come together in a satisfying balance—I quiet myself and listen. The gift of receiving ideas is something I treat with great humbleness. I know something bigger than me is at work, and that is the part of the process that I love. Something more than the sum of my thoughts—more than me—is coming up with a new unique idea or twist and restoring balance to my life. I nurture this connection by being grateful and open whenever it strikes.

I don't claim to have a firm grasp on this intangible process, but I think *that* in itself is an important realization: letting go and letting inspiration happen without needing to have control. I will never fully understand this wonderfully mystical and rewarding process called inspiration. And that is the way I like it.

2

Equilibrium
Seeking Balance

Be aware of wonder. Live a balanced life—learn some and think some and draw and paint and sing and dance and play and work every day some.

—ROBERT FULGHUM

What is "enough"?
How much is "too much"?
What consumes you?
What frees you?

Maybe you are juggling your kids' schedules with your work schedule.
Maybe others' needs always take precedence over your need for time for yourself.
Maybe your spending is more than your earnings.
Maybe you feel as if you are living your life for everyone but yourself.

To achieve balance, we need to be able to see what we have—and to sense what is missing. On a scrapbook page, this becomes a tangible reality. We can see the pieces laid out before us—color on color, shape on shape, image on image—and rearrange them as we please. We can add or take away until we are satisfied with the balance of the page. As in life, the lessons of balance come easier with practice.

Living in the Mess

The word happiness *would lose its meaning if it were not balanced by sadness.*

—CARL JUNG

Life can be tiresome and messy. On our worst days, when the emotional fog is thick like wet sand, we may try to push it aside, but it stubbornly oozes back. And we stumble along, not knowing what is wrong or what is missing, until we cry ourselves raw at a tiny emotional pinprick.

Sometimes a scrapbook page is most helpful when it tells the story of the messy and difficult side of life. Once, in a public online gallery, I saw a layout a woman had created after getting out of an abusive relationship. I gasped when I saw it, both horrified and enthralled. It included swaths of electrical tape and splotches of red paint, and it was not a pretty layout. But it was so real. I could feel her anger. She had worked through something and recorded it on this page. It would not be the page she would pull out for family birthday parties, but it was a page that expressed her truth, a page of triumph.

Sometimes we need to stop trying to make the world look beautiful and instead live with its brokenness for a little while. We need to accept the flawed as part of life's balance. A scrapbook journal can take us beyond the "pretty" to the "real," to the honest acknowledgment of the "messy" places of our lives.

Although I started out as a traditional scrapbooker using paper, tools, and my hands, I eventually switched to digital scrapbooking because I loved the ease and convenience of using

my computer. But I soon realized that my shoulders and
upper back were aching from
hours in front of the computer. My wrists were sore
from typing commands and
manipulating my mouse. And
at times, the technique, rather
than the intent of my page,
became my focus. I had lost
sight of my focal point.

I had also become reliant
on the "undo" keystroke. Any
"mess" that I created on the
computer could be undone
with the touch of a finger. Only
beautiful designs would appear on
my pages! No messes allowed.
Because I could control everything, I
felt powerful. If things got disordered,
I could clean them up completely.
People would see only what I wanted
them to see.

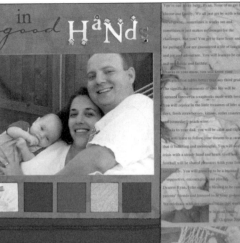

This layout has both digital and paper elements. I used computer software to create
the collage of photographs on the right-
hand side, faded them, and typed the journaling on top of them. Then, I printed it
out and added it to a paper page that
included cardstock, stamps and ink, fiber,
metal letters, and brads.

I knew it was time to rebalance. Slowly, I allowed paper elements to make their way back into my pages. I questioned myself
a lot and forced myself to commit to design choices, even if they
weren't "perfect." I felt self-conscious, slow, and cautious.

But the rewards were many! I got to use my sense of touch,
which my digital scrapbooking had neglected. I used my neck
and shoulder muscles in different ways. I stood when I worked
and stretched my legs. My hands got dirty. And I found again the
rhythm of scrapbooking, the careful selecting, the feel of paper
on my hands, the timeless moments.

Digital scrapbooking had gratified me visually, but it had
also left me wanting. The finished page lacked depth and texture.
So I returned to my supplies: smooth rhinestones, rough paper,
silky ribbons, and cool metals. When I was able to return to my

"senses," I found my balance again. When I could welcome the flaws as part of the whole, I felt alive again.

Now when I scrapbook, I use both paper and digital elements. When I feel a need for the versatility of technology, I do return to the digital page. But more often, I combine the two mediums in a new balance. A balance of mind and heart. A balance of spirit and earthiness. A balance of joy and sadness.

Each time we allow ourselves to put our lives on paper—messes and all—our scrapbooks help us rebalance our spirit and earthiness. Our joy and sadness. Our sense of what is too much and what is not enough. Our minds and hearts.

Living in the Now

I've learned that you can't have everything
and do everything at the same time.

—OPRAH WINFREY

There is lots of "stuff" involved in scrapbooking. Sometimes it is easy to get caught up in having all the best scrapbooking supplies. I spend time reading magazines and visiting scrapbook stores, and I am convinced there are a million products that will make my scrapbooking more stunning and more profound.

Scrapbooking can be a very trend-oriented activity that asserts pressure to "keep up," to do all the "right" things. I find myself looking for the latest and greatest techniques and materials, beckoned by advertising campaigns and polished marketing. I want to keep learning and experimenting, I want to see what I can accomplish, but it becomes hard to distinguish the creative impulse from the desire to fit in and be accepted, the wish to impress someone—even myself!—with my pages.

I remember a time not so long ago when I found myself consumed with thoughts and ideas for a scrapbooking contest I was planning to enter. I had hoped the contest would push me to new heights of creativity and innovation, but instead the contest seemed to be taking over my life. I found myself designing in the shower, planning colors while driving, thinking about paper choices while on the phone. I realized my spirit was being crushed by the pressure to have it all, to be the "best." I needed to find my balance again.

An effective way to rebalance is to start with what is right in front of us. We don't always need new and better materials. The better question is how we can use the materials at hand to build a page that is uniquely ours.

When I receive a page assignment from a magazine editor, I usually feel as if it justifies another trip to the scrapbooking store. I look at my current supplies and think, "They're not good enough," or "I need to start with something new." What if I had letters that were one inch taller? What if I could find a feminine floral paper that would really enhance these photos?

But, lately, I have been challenging myself to work with the paper and supplies I already own. Before looking for a new product, I try to see what I already have in new ways. What would happen if I added a subtle wash of white paint to that paper? Would that layout work if I printed out some embellishments from my digital supplies? Could I print out some letters to use in place of stickers or rub-ons?

When I do this, I find that the final product satisfies me on many levels because of the extra creativity I pour into it.

In many practical ways, scrapbooking requires that we return again and again to what we have to work with—not what we wish for, but what *is*. So it is with life. It is easy to get caught up in the dream of who we could be or what we could have or how we could change our lives. Sometimes we need to stop and become more aware of what is here, now. To take our relationships and recommit our love. To take our gifts and talents and use them in fresh ways. To take the possessions we've accumulated and value them in new ways.

To be satisfied is hard in this society where we are told to buy and improve and expand. "Too many" or "not enough" are signs that life is out of balance. The key to rebalancing is to listen and observe, to pay attention. It's interesting to note that the organ that controls our body's sense of balance is the same organ that is responsible for our sense of hearing: the ear. Balance and listening are linked. We need to be aware and alert to be balanced.

Balance, in a physical sense, "allows us to stand and walk about actively in the environment while maintaining the sense of place and direction ... and our conscious awareness of where we are and which way we are facing."[1] I think this defines spiritual balance as well. Our spiritual balance helps us know where we are and keeps our focus on what matters.

Living Creatively

Creativity takes courage.

—Henri Matisse

A lot of days I seek balance and fail. I spend too much time alone or too much time with other people. I am too active or too sedentary. I scrapbook for too many hours or I go too many days without creating anything.

Life is busy. And if I try to tell you how important it is to find time to create, your response might be, "You just don't know my life. I can't even find the time to rest, let alone create!"

Let me tell you a secret: You don't have to do it all at once. You just need to *begin*.

I've heard it said that showing up is 90 percent of life. The same is true of any creative endeavor—including scrapbooking. You don't have to wait for an entire evening to clear on your calendar. You can accomplish so much in just a few moments. Spending fifteen minutes creating—even on the busiest of days—will allow your soul to settle and a sense of balance to return.

What this *does* ask of you is to honor the value of creating, to make creating a priority. For in creating you cannot help but become more yourself. Creating brings you closer to the core of your soul.

Creating is something you can do for yourself every day, like exercising or eating chocolate or hugging the people you love. Creating every day is a way to experience yourself as being made in the image of God, the Great Creator. Creating is a way to seek balance between tasks and rewards, between work and play, between giving and receiving.

But *creativity* can be a scary word loaded with preconceived expectations of "artistry" and "inspiration," of something for a special, limited few. Even our own expectations can be a road-block to creating.

Every time I start a new scrapbook page, I am tempted to want perfection. I can become overwhelmed with the possibilities. The beauty is that, once I get started, the journey takes over as I add, take away, step back to reflect.

As the process of scrapbooking has evolved for me, I have found myself becoming more experimental and playful on paper. Instead of getting caught up in the final result, I ask myself, "What if ... ?" or "Why not ... ?" Being open to the journey of creating a page leads me to surprising vistas and feelings of accomplishment.

Once in a while, though, I find my analytical mind drifting to the outcome of a page. I start worrying about how it will look. Or I see a page in my mind and get stuck in trying to re-create it. At those moments, I take a gentle breath and remind myself to follow the path of the page—to trust my sense of balance and proportion and to allow the photographs and message to speak. I always feel better after I create in this way—more grounded and centered, cleansed and open.

Creating tames my mental jabber by getting it out of my head and into visual form. It does for my mind what exercise does for my body: creates energy, sharpens my thinking, restores my natural rhythms. Creating does for my soul what meditation does for my spirit: calms, roots, clarifies. When I'm creating, I'm tapping into the best of what it is to be human: the ability to digest and express the world around me, and the personal world within me, in tangible yet spiritual terms.

If the idea of being creative sounds a bit overwhelming, don't think *project*, think *process*. Sometimes it is helpful to focus on just one piece of the process, on one small way in which you can create a *little* bit of scrapbooking.

- Sketch layout ideas.
- Complete a step of a layout (cut out letters, stitch a background, paint the edges of photos).
- Write the journaling for a scrapbook page.
- Take photographs of anything, mindfully.
- Edit photos on your computer.

Remember: As you express yourself through color, shape, and texture on the scrapbook page, you are honoring your individual uniqueness and reflecting the image in which you were made. When you create, you are joining hands with God.

The Beauty of Balance

What I dream of is an art of balance.

—HENRI MATISSE

Balancing is an art. It is a way to embrace thinking, feeling, acting, resting, seeing, listening, and touching without being overwhelmed. I want to feel the goodness of living well-balanced days: spending time alone and time with friends, eating doughnuts and eating broccoli, enjoying the sun and walking in the moonlight, reading and writing, talking and listening.

Symmetrical balance is the simplest way to create order and beauty and is achieved when one side of an object or design is a mirror image of the other side. Symmetry is evident throughout nature. On the outside, our bodies are symmetrically balanced on a vertical line. If you drew a line from the top of the head, through the face and the chest, to the place where the legs meet and down to the toes, we are a neat mirror image of ourselves. Our skeleton has the same symmetrical balance. Nature offers other examples of symmetrical balance: flowers, insects, the wings of butterflies, seashells, animals, and the reflections of mountains in a lake.

Architecture throughout the world also employs the ease and harmony of symmetrical balance: the Taj Mahal, the White House, the Astrodome, the Leaning Tower of Pisa, and the Pantheon.[2] Many religions use symbols with symmetrical design: the Christian Cross, the Jewish Star of David, and the circular Wheel of Life of some Eastern religions. Kaleidoscopes illustrate symmetrical balance for us beautifully, captivating adults and children alike. There is something pure and holy about symmetrical balance. When we see it—in an image, in architecture, or in a life—we see beauty. We are satisfied. Symmetrical balance speaks deeply to us, to the self within us that longs for both night and day, autumn and spring, intimacy and distance.

But balance can also be asymmetrical. Our internal organs, for example, are not symmetrically balanced: stomach on one side, liver on the other, and the heart just a little off-center. Nature presents beautiful examples of asymmetrical balance in a mountain vista, the line of the horizon, and the architecture of trees.

This layout displays symmetrical balance. It is a mirror image of itself (with a bit of variety in the middle). It is settled and harmonious.

This layout shows asymmetrical balance. The photograph is balanced by the white space and words on the other side. The large faint circle is balanced by the small circle in the opposite corner.

Asymmetrical balance makes us look twice. We see a holistic unity that is not explained by a neat arrangement. Instead, it is the complexity of the display (such as a huge open blue sky contrasted against the cluttered, organic landscape) that creates interest and beauty—and at the same time, balance. Layouts with asymmetrical balance have an energetic and surprising feel.

Often when I am creating a page about a relationship, I'm struck by how many relationships are not symmetrical—people are so different, but we balance each other in beautiful ways. When I look at a picture of my grandmother and grandfather, I can't help but recall how her quiet, understated demeanor so neatly complemented his silly, gregarious spirit. Together, they just fit. The dynamic of their relationship was balanced but not symmetrical.

This is true for most of us: our lives are not symmetrical. There is no neat arrangement. But our lives can still be asymmetrically balanced, and beautifully so—like an Alexander Calder mobile. A part of our work on Earth is finding this balance on a personal level: How do I give and take? How do I make time for myself and time for others, and with others? How can my relationship with my partner encompass the gifts we both bring? How can this partnership nurture us and nurture others?

We also need to find balance on a global level: How do we take advantage of the gifts of the planet without overusing them? How do we maintain our own integrity and care for others at the same time?

When we live in balance, we take the gifts given to us and create with them a pleasing—and unexpected—composition, a composition that honors the people God intended us to be.

A BALANCING EXPERIENCE

Project: To create a scrapbook journal page that explores what you need for balance in your life.

*The best and safest thing is to keep a balance in
your life, acknowledge the great powers around us
and in us. If you can do that, and live that way,
you are really a wise [person].*

—EURIPIDES

1. Start by writing your responses to these questions:

What pulls for your attention and time?

What do you need to accomplish to feel successful?

What do you need to give to feel useful?

What do you need to take in to feel nourished?

2. Then choose elements for your page that represent the activities, pressures, responsibilities, and structure of a typical day. As you plan your page, let yourself imagine your life in balance, even if that is not the way you experience it right now. Think of how you could arrange your elements to create a physical balance on the page. The focal point of your page could be a title, such as "balance," or a photo (or group of photos) that illustrates balance.

3. Consider whether you want symmetrical or asymmetrical balance on your page. Although a symmetrical balance is easier, it is more likely that a page with asymmetrical balance will illustrate the dynamic of your life. Asymmetrical balance is far more interesting and complex. The goal with asymmetrical balance is to achieve harmony on a page that is not predictable.

2-1

2-2

2-3

Here are some possibilities:

- *Use one large element with several small elements. (See layout 2-1.)*

- *Pair a dominant photograph with white space (unused, blank space on any part of your layout). (See layout 2-2.)*

- *Utilize a visual triangle of items of similar color, shape, or value. On layout 2-3, note the similarity in the circular shapes in the title strip, the shape of the tree's root ball, and the circles below the word gifts.*

- *Work with areas divided into thirds (⅔ and ⅓, or ⅓, ⅓, and ⅓) instead of halves. (See layout 2-4.)*

- *Evenly distribute color around the page. (We'll talk more about color in chapter 6.)*

4. Once you have an idea in mind, draw a quick sketch if that helps you. It is not necessary to plan all the details, just to start with an intentional idea. You can add other embellishments or supporting images as you work. Creating is a process, and you might be surprised by what appears on the journey.

5. Begin your page. Use whatever mediums please you: paint, paper, stitching, stamps, markers, stickers, digital technology. Be open to creative ideas as they come. Even though you started with a rough plan, your page will evolve as you work. Add photos, words (people's names, places, things, verbs and actions, or a mixture), and embellishments that depict the elements in your life.

6. Keep aiming for a balanced page. Think of your page as hovering above your workspace, with its very center balanced on the tip of a pencil. The term *visual weight*

describes the heaviness that certain elements bring. As you add elements, keep this heaviness balanced.

2-4

When you're aiming for balance, proportion is not far behind.

Proportion is the difference in size between items. The right proportion can create visual harmony. Keep proportion in mind by using enough contrast in size to be interesting, but not so much that one item looks out of place.

Add and take away elements until you are satisfied with the page. As you work, remember to balance shapes, colors, and textures. Remember to bring attention to the focal point of the page.

7. When you sense that your page portrays how you would like the balance of your life to be, give yourself some reflection time.

> *What does the page tell you?*
>
> *Does any element stand out? What elements have a primary role? A supporting role?*
>
> *Does your page feel crowded or is there enough space?*
>
> *Is there anything that needs to go? Is there anything that seems lacking?*
>
> *What would you like to add or take away?*
>
> *What parallels are there between the page and your life?*
>
> *Is your body getting enough attention?*
>
> *Is your mind getting enough stimulation?*
>
> *Is your spirit finding enough meaning and fulfillment?*
>
> *What are some things the page tells you about what needs rebalancing in your life?*

If you'd like to see how Katja Kromann and I interpreted this balance exercise, see the two "Balance" layouts on the color insert.

Going Deeper

Additional exercises in balance.

Don't hold on too long,
but don't let go too soon. Find a balance.

—MORRIE SWARTZ

✳ Create a layout with symmetrical balance (vertical or horizontal).

✳ Create a layout with asymmetrical balance.

✳ Create a scrapbook page about a relationship in your life that balances you.

✳ If you are a digital scrapbooker, try to include some traditional elements on your next page. Some ideas: Print out your page and then add ribbon or stitching. Create a digital collage with a title, then print it out and add patterned paper and flowers.

✳ If you are an entirely traditional scrapbooker, try to include some digital elements. Some ideas: Add brushes to your photos before printing them. Add journaling text to your photos. Print your journaling on cardstock and add it to your layout. Print out brushes on a transparency and adhere it on top of your layout. Use a computer to change the size of your photos, then print them or have them printed.

✳ Create a page describing how you seek balance in your life. What strategies do you use to help achieve balance (exercise, dinner-sharing, babysitter, meditation/prayer, etc.)?

Notes ————

A Voice along the Journey

I started scrapbooking January 20, 1985. I remember the date because I wrote it in my journal. I was only ten years old. With my Spirograph kit, I made a design I was proud of, cut it out, and pasted it in my journal. I immediately fell in love with the idea of preserving my pictures in a book, and from that day forward I've been hooked on scrapbooking.

When I was in junior high, my parents gave me a long folding table to put in my room and a magnetic scrapbook album. Looking back, I think that was the best gift they could have ever given me. I spent a lot of time at that table, writing in my journal, coloring with my scented markers, and scrapbooking. I didn't scrapbook many of my own pictures; instead, I created pages about what I liked and what was important to me. Scrapbooking gave me the time to meditate and focus on the things I wanted to remember in life. I had a desire to record my life on paper and didn't want those pages to be filled with regret. The time I spent scrapbooking and writing in my journal helped me find myself—and become closer to God.

My scrapbooks are my favorite possessions. I love looking back at them. I believe they continue to help me discover who I really am. They help me feel good about what I've done in my life, and they help me remember the things I want to be doing to achieve the goals I have set for myself. The pages are not only a link to my past, but they also help form my future. In a way, I choose my actions based on the way I want the book of my life to be written. Through my scrapbook pages, I can see how I have grown over the years—not only physically, but emotionally and spiritually as well.

3

Movement
Encouraging Growth

*The greatest thing in this world
is not so much where we stand
as in what direction we are moving.*

—OLIVER WENDELL HOLMES

What do you hold on to?
What seems to hold on to you?
Where do you sense your life is heading?
In which ways do you want to grow?

Maybe the daily routine of your life has grown stale and you
wonder what's missing.

Maybe you sense a growing urge to try something you've
never tried before.

Maybe you feel as if the people who depend on you are holding you back—or your own fears are keeping you from
moving forward.

Maybe the familiarity of what you know is more attractive
than the risk of the unknown.

Life is movement. Some of it is the good stuff—growth and learning and excitement—and much of it is the difficult stuff—like forgiveness and grief and letting go. Movement teaches us about ourselves. It also teaches us how to be closer to God, because movement reminds us that we need God for stability and strength. Movement gives birth to faith.

In a way, scrapbooking is a metaphor for life's movement. As a craft or practice, scrapbooking inherently involves surprises, things we didn't expect to happen on the page, things that ask us to let go of the original plan. Scrapbooking also means learning new techniques and varying the routine, moving on to other forms and possibilities. And, most important, experimenting with change on a scrapbook page teaches us about embracing change in our lives.

Letting Go

When one door closes, another opens.

—ALEXANDER GRAHAM BELL

"John ..." I said slowly, "where are the files that used to be on the P drive? Did you move them?"

"No, I deleted them," he said. "That's why you backed them up on your external hard drive, right?"

I felt a flash of fear. "No ... I just copied the files from my laptop. But all of my old files—layouts, journaling, and projects—were on the desktop, and I didn't copy those."

"I really thought we had talked about me deleting them. I needed to make more space."

I remembered the conversation about needing more space on our desktop computer. As I recall, he told me something about partitioning, gigabytes, and backups, and he said he would be moving everything except pictures to a different drive. At the time I thought, "No problem. My stuff will be safe wherever it goes ... no matter what the drive is called."

But a month later I was looking for a piece of journaling on the desktop and the files were no longer there. A quiet sense of loss overcame me. So many files representing so much—gone. Scans of the pages of the scrapbook I made for good friends, scans of the pages of the book I made for my dear friend Tammy, for her thirtieth birthday ... gone. Every album I'd ever made for a gift ... all the journaling I'd written on the computer ... all the components of layouts and sketches ... all gone.

It was a strange feeling. I knew that somewhere in the world the tangible projects lived on. But they were no longer mine; I could not hold on to them any longer. I didn't cry. I just felt a dull sadness tempered by a strange peace.

Over and over again, <u>life asks us to let go</u>. The seasons remind us that everything changes. Our relationships demand that we let individuals be who they are, at any given time, and accept the good and the bad qualities together. The cycle of life and aging and death requires that we release our compulsion to control time. Tension in our muscles—a tightness of control—is a sign that we are holding on too tightly to schedules or burdens or time itself.

We are always learning the lesson of letting go, and the process of scrapbooking offers us multiple opportunities to practice. On one level, we know that we will ultimately have to let go of our scrapbooks just as we will have to let go of our lives. Albums can be destroyed by fire or flood—or by the simple deterioration of digital prints or adhesives. Even as we try to preserve special moments, we are reminded that they are every bit as tenuous and fragile as life.

On another level, the creation of each scrapbook page can be a mini-lesson in letting go. Recently, I was completing a layout for a design team submission. I had printed a photo collage onto photo paper, trimmed it, sewn a frame and title, and adhered the collage to cardstock and patterned paper. I had attached ribbons and stamped and applied rub-ons.

Then it happened. I was careless with the rub-on. And a small but noticeable curve appeared near a face on one of my photographs. It made the shape of a bird ... the kind kids (and I, still) draw in their skies. Two little humps. Absolutely out of place. So I stopped for a minute, considered, and reconsidered: Could I redo this layout in time? Was it worth it to redo? Somehow I

could not talk myself into starting over. This inconsequential 8½-inch square layout—a tiny slice of my life—and a smudge of rub-on was just not that important.

"I think you just need to go with it," John suggested. I had tons of rub-ons left. So I began rubbing. And I created flowers where there had been none before. They curved around the photograph and ended at the title, focusing on the focal point, adding a softness to the layout. Was I 100 percent pleased with the outcome? No. But I was pleased that I could let go of my original plan and make way for the new opportunities that emerged. In a small but very real way, I could see that by letting go of "shoulds" and expectations, I made room for the unexpected gift.

Letting go may sound like an emptying process, but it is really a key to living fully. Letting go is the doorway to surprises, the road to new discoveries, and a channel for blessings we never expected.

Embracing the Ebb and Flow

Change has a considerable psychological impact on the human mind. To the fearful it is threatening because it means that things may get worse. To the hopeful it is encouraging because things may get better. To the confident it is inspiring because the challenge exists to make things better.

—KING WHITNEY JR.

When I was little, we moved a lot. My dad was in the Air Force, so every few years the announcement would come: it was time to move on. My sister and I would meet this announcement with much anguish and tears, but I think part of me didn't mind. Moving meant change, something new and exciting, an adventure.

Even now, when I get a call from our supervisor at work saying we need to have a meeting, part of me is secretly happy. Usually we're going to hear about some policy or personnel change—something that will mix up our life for a few days, give us something to talk about, and propel us forward to new growth. Change is necessary. Movement keeps us from getting bored and makes way for gifts beyond what we could imagine.

But change can be a tough companion. I see the fear of change often in our work as Teaching-Parents. The girls we live with tend to resist change—even when the change is good. The other day, one of them said to me, "I'm scared to get too close to you and John because I might have to leave." So many of our girls come to us with this fear and have no way to express it except by pushing us away. I was so grateful she could say it aloud.

I told her we considered it a great privilege to get to know and love the girls who walked through our lives—even with the constant certainty that they were taking steps, every day, toward leaving us.

And I told her about my life when I was growing up. How I had become used to grasping on to a place, then letting go when we moved every three years or so. How I learned that one of the greatest things we can do is let people in, even knowing that they might not stay.

Although I may encourage our girls about change, I certainly don't always welcome it myself. For the first few years that I scrapbooked, I *always* created a double-page spread on 12 x 12-inch pages. The two pages offered a wide expanse and consistency throughout my albums. Whenever I sat down to create a page, I would begin by rote with my two squares of cardstock. I liked the familiar.

8½ x 8½-inch layout

But as I began to be more playful with scrapbooking, I found myself drawn to other page layouts. What about a single 12 x 12-inch page? Or two 8½ x 11-inch pages? What about a mini-book (5 x 5 inches or so)? Why not let each layout call for its own amount of space? Why not experiment?

So I did. Yes, it makes a mess in my albums. Facing pages no longer match. I have albums that are 12 x 12, 8½ x 8½, and 8½ x 11 inches. Then there is a whole little cluster of messy mini-books, with ribbons poking out the sides. The uniformity may be gone, but each page is more meaningful and focused. And every new page size offers new opportunities, new ways to play with balance and to emphasize the focal point.

12 x 12-inch layout (two facing pages)

pink lights, and purple & silver bulbs. But these ornaments are from my history.

dec 23

We have not yet established an ornament collection in our home - our tree is a girlish combination of fake pearls,

memories

Ornaments

5 x 7-inch layout (two facing pages)

An interesting thing happens when you allow a little change. One change opens the door to another, inviting something new in each time. Sometimes the results are chaos; sometimes the experiment works. Most important, when things get turned upside down, you can sometimes see them in a new way. You can discover new ideas, new opportunities that you hadn't thought about before. It is only as we move through the messiness of change that we move toward spiritual wholeness. Embracing the ebb and flow of our lives is fundamental for our sense of spiritual purpose.

These are the faces of 2004.
Faces that change us
Faces that keep us the same
New fresh unknown faces
Faces more familiar than our own
Faces of three sweet baby boys
Faces lined with wrinkles of time and wisdom
Faces smooth and soft and young
Furry purring faces
Faces exploding with joy
Faces pouring out tears
Faces that challenge us
Faces that comfort us
Faces that bring smiles

These are the faces we love.

(Our faces: at the Conservatory in San Francisco, April; catching a sunset while shopping for a couch, April; dancing at our friends' wedding, June; relaxing on a hammock while visiting friends in Memphis, September; dressed up for Halloween party with our girls, October; in Cleveland for the International Teaching Family Association Conference, November.)

8½ x 11-inch layout

Growing through the Rough Times

Turbulence is life force. It is opportunity.
Let's love turbulence and use it for change.

—RAMSAY CLARK

There's one thing we all know about movement: somewhere along the line there will be grieving, forgiving, mourning, releasing. There will be dark times along with the times of celebration. There will be times when we discover our inner strengths, and times when we will know our need for God.

Growth means embracing every moment, not just the fantastically exciting or stimulating ones. It also means accepting sadness and disappointment as part of life, and embracing the gifts that struggle and time will bring.

I doubt the day will come when I welcome difficult times with the same joy I welcome celebrations. When sadness creeps into my life, my first instinct is to squash it. Find more happiness. Look on the bright side. But the longer I live, the more I see that sadness is as much a part of life as happiness is. Life—a full life— is about both.

Sometimes my sadness is not something I can attribute to a specific cause, but is more a feeling of emptiness. There are times when I just seem to lose my motivation or inspiration. I don't have any desire to follow through with the project that had been brewing in my mind just a week before. Some days I feel that nothing I can make or do will be good enough or inspiring enough or beautiful enough.

The best advice I've ever heard about overcoming depression or insecurity is, "*Do* something." Do something for yourself or for another person—even for the houseplants! It doesn't really matter what it is; the act of *doing* will help.

The worst days for me are when I sit and think too much about what I could be doing or what I should be doing or what is missing. But as soon as I start *doing* something, my feelings begin to shift. I start to feel productive. I stop looking at what is missing and start seeing what I just created: a cleaner house, a birthday card, a loaf of bread, an e-mail to a friend, a scrapbook page.

Scrapbooking is a great impetus to do something. In the act of creating a page, there must be photographs (taken by you), supplies (organized by you), and design (developed by you). When a page is finished, it is a visible sign not only of the moment you documented, but also of the energy and love you gave to the creating.

When you feel creatively paralyzed (maybe you haven't scrapbooked

A journal page of self-expression during a difficult time for me.

for a while, or are struggling with difficult emotions, or are just doubting your abilities), you can start within the privacy of your journal. Instead of jumping into a full-blown scrapbook page, begin with a photograph that resonates with you, and start writing your thoughts and feelings about it. Or just write what is on your mind and add stamps or doodles around it.

Your topic might be about you or someone else. It might be emotional or intellectual. But no matter the topic, as you relax into the process, it will awaken a creative spark that will evolve naturally into your next "public" page.

Gaining Perspective

The first step toward change is awareness.

—Nathaniel Branden

I love to travel, especially if I get to fly somewhere. I always request a window seat so I can see what is happening as we take off and land. Sometimes I get lucky and fly on a clear day when I can see the Earth sprawled below me. It is magical. I've always loved maps and the shapes of the land, and to be able to move far enough away from the surface to see it all at once—to recognize borders and roads and bodies of water—is amazing.

I may be the only person on the plane who uses the little maps in the back of the airline's free travel magazine. They are especially helpful if they have those little arched lines showing where the plane travels. But sometimes they don't, and I have to deduce my location from the position of the sun and the shapes on the Earth below.

On a recent trip to Mexico, we flew near a body of land that definitely was not in the United States. Looking at the map and out the window, I figured that the land was Cuba, and I felt a tinge of awe. Cuba seems so forbidden and exotic, and to be able to see it out my window was a moment of triumph and satisfactory sneakiness. On the way back we looked out over Florida, which was almost as satisfying, since I actually recognized it. Plus, we had lived there when I was in high school, and I could see the shapes of the land that were once so familiar to me: the western coast, the arching Tampa Bay, the sprawling suburbs and bridge spans. How awesome to see a meaningful place from afar.

Scrapbooking can give us this kind of perspective. Here we are, immersed in the experience of our lives, caught up and busy and focused. But when we stop to scrapbook, we take a step back and get a different view. When we arrange the pieces of our lives on the page, we can see the contours of our days and the shape of our lives from a unique vantage point. Ordinary events can strike us with their beauty and breadth. We can see the movement in our lives. And we can give thanks.

Sometimes scrapbooking takes us into unfamiliar spaces, too. We look at photographs and try to remember who we were, once. Or who the people we loved were. And we connect the dots, creating the borders of a map of our lives.

At a recent dinner gathering with my grandparents, my mom pulled out some old photographs: Grandma and Grandpa on their wedding day, Grandma with her college roommates, Mom as a baby taking a bath, Mom and her siblings posing for a studio photograph. I paged through them while my grandmother told me some of the stories that went along with them. I know she has many more photographs and stories. One of my hopes is that I'll be able to sit down with her on a quiet afternoon, look through the photographs, and write down the stories. She will talk and smile and I'll take notes, hungry for her perspective and experiences, knowing that in many ways we are connected, that her stories are also the earliest stories of my life.

These shared moments impel me to write down my story now—to create scrapbook pages so that one day my grand-daughter and I can look through the albums together. So that I will have the chance to talk and smile and remember, and share.

I'll tell her the story of my time alone. I love to walk through the forest at a local park. Nothing fancy—just time alone with music and nature and myself. I want her to know about the importance of carving out time to spend alone in replenishing activities. She will not have to write down my stories, but can write her own, about the stories we create together.

There is something comforting about having these kinds of pages in our albums, within our homes. When we are consumed by what is happening right now, it is easy to forget about who and what came before, to lose the larger perspective. But each of us has a story that extends further back than we can see, a story that began before we were alive and will continue long after we pass away.

A GROWING EXPERIENCE

Project: To create a scrapbook journal page to help you understand more fully a significant change—either positive or negative—in your life.

Life is change. Growth is optional. Choose wisely.

—KAREN KAISER CLARK

1. Pick one event, conversation, or relationship that has changed you in some way. It can be small or large, universal or very personal. Then write your responses to these questions:

    How did it happen?

    What were the immediate effects?

    Where did it lead you?

    How did it change you?

    When you look back on it, what are you grateful for about the change?

june 2005

S&P

after · two · years

After two years of marriage, Sarah & Pete know exactly how to pose for pictures together... they wear color-coordinated outfits without planning to ...and everyone around them can tell they are still in love

3-1

2. Then choose the basic elements for your page. What will convey your experience? Photographs? Drawings? A title? A quotation? A word or letters?

3. Then begin to think of how you can show movement on your page to reflect your changes. Here are some techniques you might consider:

- *Use a visual triangle (three spots on your layout that are similar in color or shape). The brain will connect those three spots and the eye will move easily across the page. For example, on layout 3-1 the swirling motif is repeated in three places.*

- *Create a horizontal line across the page to draw the eye naturally from left to right. This can be done with ribbon, strips of paper, strips of color, lines of text, elements within the photographs, or a line of accents. For example, on layout 3-2 I used elements within the photograph (the strong line of the horizon and pattern of the geese), as well as journaling that moves*

my place

I don't know why I so love this poem by Mary Oliver. Maybe it is the imagery of nature. Maybe the suggestion of connections. Or the message of hope. Or the permission to be exactly who I am, at this moment, without being sorry or anxious or alone. But it speaks to me . . . like the geese . . . helping me find my home. Helping me find my place in this world.

Wild Geese

You do not have to be good.
You do not have to walk on
your knees for a hundred miles
through the desert, repenting.
You only have to let the soft
animal of your body love what
it loves.
Tell me about despair, yours,
and I will tell you mine.
Meanwhile the world goes on.
Meanwhile the sun and the clear
pebbles of the rain are moving
across the landscapes,
over the prairies and deep
trees, the mountains and the
rivers.
Meanwhile the wild geese, high in
the clean blue air
are heading home again.
Whoever you are, no matter how
lonely, the world offers itself to
your imagination, calls to you like
the wild geese, harsh and exciting--
over and over announcing your
place in the family of things.

3-2

across the page, to create a sense of movement. You can also create a vertical line on the page in a similar way. A vertical line tends to convey more energy and dynamism than a horizontal line does.

• Use shapes such as circles or diamonds. Curving elements such as rub-ons or circles will especially help the eye move across the page. (See layout 3-3.)

• Use repetition. Repeat shapes, colors, and textures across the page. At first you might think repetition is a strange way to communicate movement. Movement makes us think of change and differences, of contrast and variety, while repetition makes us think of standing still. But if you think about it, repetition has its own movement. In the repeated elements—whether of nature or rituals or routines—we gain a broader sense of motion. When the seasons cycle round again, or the sun rises every morning, we are reminded that life is moving forward. When the family gathers for a familiar evening meal, we are aware that yet another day is drawing to a close. Even the ordinary repeated routines—paying bills, renewing magazine subscrip-

tions, stocking up at the grocery store (again)—remind us that life is moving on. Just as the repeated elements of life slowly propel us forward, so, too, the repeated elements on the scrapbook page carry us along. (See layout 3-4.)

- *Arrange your photographs in a linear fashion across the page, as I did on layout 3-5. You can also arrange them in a more free-form sweeping line (curved or swirling). This works especially well for two-page layouts.*

3-3

4. Once you have some ideas in mind, draw a quick sketch, if that helps you. Remember to consider what you will use to emphasize your focal point: size? contrast? line? color? a combination of these? Start with an intentional idea but leave room for surprises. You can add other embellishments or supporting images as you work.

3-4

5. Begin your page. Use whatever mediums please you: paint, paper, stitching, stamps, markers, stickers, digital technology. Be open to creative ideas as they come. Even though you started with a rough plan, your page will evolve as you work.

6. Include your thoughts in the form of journaling. Explore this question:

How did this event or conversation lead you to become who and how you are today?

3-5

7. As you work, keep returning to your main idea, the focal point. Check to ensure that you are creating a sense of movement. Let the process flow.

8. When you are satisfied with your exploration of this change and movement in your life, give yourself time to reflect on these questions:

> *What elements carry the eye across the page? How does that relate to what carries you through in your life experience?*
>
> *Is there any place where something seems stuck or incomplete? What can you learn from this? In what ways is your soul asking to grow?*
>
> *What have you learned from this change?*
>
> *What lessons does this change still hold for you?*

If you'd like to see how April Oaks and I interpreted this growing exercise, see "This Changes Me" and "It Happened Here" on the color insert.

Going Deeper

Additional exercises in personal growth.

> *I can't change the direction of the wind, but I can adjust my sails to always reach my destination.*
>
> —JIMMY DEAN

✳ Create a scrapbook page that gives three snapshots of your life: now, five years ago, and five years from now. Divide your page into three sections and include photos and journaling in each that illustrate the person you have been and are becoming.

✳ Create a scrapbook page about someone you have loved who is no longer in your life (because of death, breakup, or geography). Write about the lessons you learned from knowing that person and how your relationship helped you grow.

✳ Make a mini-scrapbook that documents this week in your life. Look for a lesson in each day. Then step back and view the movement of the week. Where did you start? Where did the week take you?

✳ Look through a current scrapbook magazine (see Appendix B for suggestions) and find a technique you have not yet tried. Use it on your next scrapbook page. Give yourself the chance to explore something new.

✳ Think of your most recent journey—either physical, such as a trip or a move, or a journey of learning or growth—and create a scrapbook journal page to document the process. For example, I created a scrapbook journal to document the process of writing this book.

A Voice along the Journey

JESSICA SPRAGUE

Of all the things I've learned from scrapbooking, perhaps the most surprising is the awareness I have gained about my own parents. I have begun to see the personalities and motivations and love from the people behind the camera for all those years of my childhood.

This sense of connectedness has come as I've learned to value the small moments of life, to relish in my interaction with my own kids, to see the parallels in my relationship with my parents. For instance, my parents tell the story (with laughter in their voices) of how as a toddler I used to get up on hands and knees and rub my nose across the carpet, laughing because of the attention I got. Recently, I discovered a photo of myself at that age, sitting on the floor, wrinkling my nose at someone off to the left of the camera. Suddenly the story sprang to life, not only as my story, but theirs as well. I understood their delight, and how they must have run for the camera when I started my "routine," because that's exactly what I do with my kids now.

I'm thankful that my parents understood the value of photos: precious capsules of times past, but remembered forever. They knew what I'm just now learning: that what is captured in a photo—the Christmases and birthdays and family vacations—are valuable, but, more important, it is our connection with family and friends, the record of our story, that matters. Every time I run for the camera to capture the antics and joy of my own kids, I think about my mom and dad, and feel a little more of the love and joy that make a family.

4

Awareness
Enlarging Your Vision

Vision is the art of seeing the invisible.

—JONATHAN SWIFT

What do you see?
What do you perceive?
What do you imagine?
What do you want to create?

There are three kinds of visual images: what we observe, what we imagine, and what we create.[1] The three images are different yet overlapping, and the beauty of scrapbooking is that it combines all three. When we scrapbook, we begin with what we observe—we capture what we see in photographs. Then we record our deeper observations in our writing. Our minds imagine a home for these observations, and we begin the process of creating—the powerful ability to combine inspiration and imagination, the most divinely human skill of artistic expression.

Discovering Beauty

Those who look for beauty, find it.

—UNKNOWN

I've always been drawn to photography over other visual arts. Some think photography is unimaginative because you can't create a photograph out of nothingness, as you can with a blank canvas and pastels or watercolors. But there is something magical about photography: it requires that we find the beauty that already exists in the world and capture it. We create with what we are already given. It is an art of gratitude.

The word *photography* literally means "writing with light." We often think of light as a static presence that varies depending on the time of day. But what if we remember that light is always in motion? It is the fastest traveler. And when it arrives at us, we absorb some of it and we reflect some of it—giving those around us a glimpse of who we are. Light illuminates. It helps us see what really is.

As I've grown older, my visual acuity has increased. Not physically—I've become more and more nearsighted as each year passes—but spiritually—life stuns me more and more with its beauty. Things I would have walked by fifteen years ago—a striking flower, the sun sparkling on water, a photograph of the light reflected in someone's eyes—stop me now. Sometimes we get so accustomed to something that we no longer "see" it—let alone see the beauty in it. Photography sharpens our sense of sight and helps us rediscover the beauty we've missed.

And scrapbooking nurtures our sense of sight further. When photographs are trapped inside albums or boxes, we glance through them quickly. We notice faces or environments, and we keep flipping. But a scrapbook page begs us to stop. It says, "Look. Here. This matters right now. Do you see how beautiful this moment was … and is?"

We are scrapbookers because we love photographs. There is a truth and a presence in them that assure us of something.

Something we long to clasp and save. Something we cannot put into words.

A year ago my husband and I took a trip to meet friends at a cabin in the Blue Ridge Mountains. We arrived several hours before our friends, and we were immediately charmed by the cabin. Well over a hundred years old, it was a log cabin with chinking in the cracks, a wood-burning stove, and a narrow stairway to the loft. It was nestled in a small clearing in the middle of the woods. September had just begun; summer was saying goodbye, but the sunshine was still warm and welcoming. After settling into our accommodations, I walked outside with my camera and began capturing photographs of our surroundings. Pink and red impatiens graced window boxes on either side of the old oak front door. A crooked split-rail fence drew my eye in a line toward a rustic shed. Wildflowers dotted the green bushes and trees on the edge of the clearing. A stone patio absorbed the sun's warmth and made a home for two Adirondack chairs, waiting for dear friends to settle in and reconnect.

These few minutes of photographing the environment set the stage for the warmth of the weekend to come. It gave me an appreciation for the beauty of our surroundings and a chance to focus on the pleasing environment that someone had created. The experience was meditative. It took me outside myself for a

few minutes and made the rustic beauty so clear. And by the time our friends arrived, I felt as if our surroundings were waiting to embrace our laughter and intimacy.

Weeks later, when I prepared to create a scrapbook page of our mountain gathering, I realized that, though the photographs of the cabin were secondary to my friends' faces and smiles, they needed a place on the page, too.

Photography and scrapbooking teach us to embrace our environment. So often we zoom forward and don't take time to allow our sense of sight to savor what surrounds us. But photography invites us to slow down and pay attention. Then, as we move on to create a scrapbook page, we can appreciate and enjoy the true beauty of our connection with nature and each other.

Discovering Others

Beauty is not in the face; beauty is a light
in the heart.

—KHALIL GIBRAN

Someone recently told me that I had missed my true calling and that I should have been a photographer. She said I captured the personality of one of my girls, Eva, much better than the professional photographer whom they had hired the previous month. I know she is wrong about my true calling—I possess neither the skill nor the equipment to be a professional photographer. But one of the reasons I could take beautiful pictures of Eva is because I *know* her. I *know* how beautiful she is, inside and out.

When you know someone—really know and love him or her—it is a special gift to be on the viewing side of the camera. I love watching and recording the moments as the girls in my life grow into women. I love witnessing God hold their hands through adolescence, knowing that they will walk their own paths.

One of our girls, Michelle, who is now eighteen, came to live with us when she was just fourteen. I love looking at pictures of her throughout her years here. We have pictures of her in the Blue Ridge Mountains on her first hike, tentatively posing with her hands on a tree. We have pictures of her in her first work uniform, ready to take new steps to independence. We have pictures of her in her homecoming dress, at first shy and unsmiling, then beaming and confident. (I had to stop the photo session and show her the digital images of her on my camera to convince her that she looked stunning, and evoke that smile from her.) And we will have pictures of her graduating from high school, white-robed and hopeful. All these pictures make visible the young adolescent, once argumentative and scared and skeptical, who has blossomed into a young woman, confident and caring and agreeable. Photographs are gifts that portray these important times of change.

And photographs contain the core of our relationships. If someone is looking at my camera, our relationship is held in that space between camera and eyes. There is an intimate moment that occurs when people let us view them purposefully, through a camera lens. Any authentic emotion that we can capture comes from their reaction to us.

I treasure close-up photographs of the people I love. It is the beginning of satisfying my desire to know them deeply. I think of my father. I may never be able to have the depth of conversation that I would like with him, but I can take photographs that capture his essence: his wise smile and warm blue eyes, the familiar shape of his head. These photographs give me the tiniest glimmer of insight into who he really is.

When we take a picture of someone, we are saying, "I see you. I behold you." Not just in a visual sense, but in a spiritual sense. We are saying, "This moment matters. You, in this moment, matter. Can I preserve this?" Photographs make time stand still and heighten our awareness. They help us love the moment—and each other.

So often I move quickly—taking care of details, making plans, accomplishing tasks—and don't take time to appreciate the person who is right in front of me. Or maybe I'm too shy to say to loved ones how I feel about the experience of just sitting with them, observing their beauty, and being grateful for their presence in my life. But once I have my photographs and am alone in my space, I can slow down and celebrate. I linger over the photographs and write. After a recent visit with my longtime friend Amy, I wrote this journaling that eventually became a scrapbook page. (Notice that I wrote the journaling as if it were a letter addressed to her. When I create a page, I find it helps me be more intimate and true if I write directly to the subject, instead of about him or her.)

You asked me to take some pictures of you for work, and I was thrilled! So we escaped for a little bit, found a sunlit window, and started snapping away. I didn't like any of the pictures. I adjusted the window blinds. I had you reposition your chair. I took some more. You took off your shoes to get more comfortable. I had you pose with the cat. We laughed. And then Ryan woke up from his nap, and our husbands decided we all needed to get out of the house. We resigned ourselves to some mediocre

pictures, and we hoped to get back to the photo shoot. Well, we didn't. So these are the pictures I have. And the thing is, now, I love them. In our busy weekend visit, we did not get too many moments alone. This moment was kind of awkward and some-what rushed, but it was ours. And now I have these pictures to remind me of all the things about you that I love but cannot take a picture of: your enthusiasm, your devotion, your vulnerability, your faith. Amy, you are a gift in my life. I am so grateful for every moment with you!

If we let them, photographs can remind us of the essence of the people we love. A stranger might not see the beauty we see, but friendship gives us the gift of sight. Linger over your photographs. Let them guide you toward seeing the depth of compassion and gratitude and grace that resides within the people you love. As you collect these photographs onto your scrapbook pages, celebrate the important people in your life.

Discovering Yourself

Your vision will become clear only when you look into your heart. Who looks outside, dreams. Who looks inside, awakens.

—CARL JUNG

Are you one of those people who hates to have her picture taken? Do you feel as if the camera never captures the appearance that you would like to present to the world? I used to dread picture day at school. I'd sit awkwardly posed and uncomfortable, lifting my chin and forcing a smile … only to see the disappointing results weeks later.

It doesn't help that we are pummeled with images of artificial beauty—tanning-bed-darkened skin, airbrushed thighs, and smiles of artificially white teeth. Our culture surrounds us with these images in the hopes of winning our money and time and loyalty. The allure of perfection is inescapable. The comparison game begins.

But I find that I win the game a lot quicker if I focus on *sameness* rather than *differences*. Instead of looking at the ways I am *different* from these glorified images of beauty, I look at the ways I am the *same* as the people I love. I may not have the cheekbones of a model, but I have the same soft cheeks and jaw as one of my favorite aunts. My smile, which one of my fourth-grade students told me shows a little too much gum (and not enough teeth) is a gift from my mom. And my sun-loving skin, which will never be flawless alabaster, comes straight from my father. So when I look in a mirror, or see a photograph of myself, I see an artful combining of all these qualities. These are gifts from my family, every bit as much as the gifts of time and love and wisdom that got me through childhood and beyond. They have combined to make me uniquely me.

So I don't mind pictures of myself now. More and more, I am able to recognize my own kind of beauty in them. After thirty-three years, I am finally glimpsing what God intended.

Many scrapbookers I know have a difficult time making pages of themselves. They focus on preserving the lives of their children and spouse and extended relatives, but don't easily stand on the other side of the camera or take time to honor pictures of themselves. But this step of self-preservation is important. In creating a page about yourself, you can begin to see the gift God intends you to be—a gift to yourself and a gift to the world.

Since my early twenties I've had blotchy skin. It seemed to come out of nowhere, but looking back I could trace it to the years of sun exposure: teenage years (living near the beach) and college years (working at an outdoor summer camp). It was hard to accept at first. I felt unfeminine and ugly, unpolished and harsh. As the years passed, I became more diligent with moisturizer and sunscreen, and grew to embrace hats and the shade, which I can only imagine has helped somewhat. But still, the blotches remained....

Then one day I started finding photographs of myself outside, in the sunshine. Starting from my toddler years, when I would go camping with my parents, up through my high school trips with friends to the beach, on to college years of hiking the Appalachian Trail and rafting down rivers, and finally, now, recent trips to Cancun and to San Francisco, and joyful outings in our little orange convertible. As I looked at the pile of photographs, I realized what they all have in common: my sheer pleasure in being outside, in feeling the sun on my face and the wind on my skin. Nothing soothes me in quite the same way. It is one of the ways I feel close to God and at peace with myself. I am not willing to sacrifice that time outside—or the memories of my adventures—for prettier skin. So I gathered the photographs and started writing down my thoughts.

By the time I finished collecting pictures and writing the journaling to accompany them, the scrapbook page I created was no longer about my skin. It was about the way I see life and the gifts I will not sacrifice. It is a page I can look at on my bad days, and realize that I am living the life I want to live … and that I have to gracefully accept the consequences of the life I've chosen.

Photography, and the process of honoring those photographs in our scrapbook pages, can help us accept ourselves. As Thomas Moore observes in *Dark Nights of the Soul,*

> *Photography is a contemporary art form that has an extraordinary capacity to reveal the hidden soul. In a photograph you see things that pass by unnoticed in the flow of life … and the jarring of a photograph can wake you up to a new interpretation of who you were and what you have become.*[2]

Expanding Your Vision

The greatest thing a human soul ever does in this world is to see something…. To see clearly is poetry, prophecy, and religion, all in one.

—JOHN RUSKIN

Today I met with my friend Lucy and we talked about photography. Lucy has an amazing knowledge of native plants, and she loves to photograph wildflowers. She sets out on hikes and only covers the first quarter mile because she is so busy bending and

It was a beautiful day when I visited Lucy at Camp Hanover in autumn. Warm fall day. Bright sun and blue sky. We walked the labyrinth then took our familiar hike. We talked about photography and family and art and nature. So grateful for this day!

October 2005

A layout I created after spending a day hiking, talking, and taking photographs with my friend Lucy.

crouching and looking and capturing. The flowers captivate her, and she has to record an image of them.

I asked her, "What does taking photographs do to you? What does it feel like?"

She told me the story of a time around Thanksgiving when she was taking a hike with her family. She enjoyed the hike but felt somewhat distant and unsettled. As her family walked ahead, she stopped along the path for a moment and took pictures of a teaberry plant. She crouched down low and took in the details, letting that tiny plant fill her moment. Looking through her lens, she could see the intricacies of the plant. She could see God's gift in its tiniest form. And as she rose to stand, after capturing a few frames, her spirit was transformed. Looking through the lens had changed something in her. Looking at the immaculate details of the plant had soothed her and nourished her. It had awed her. It had centered her.

Photography is an opening. We begin taking photographs to capture a moment, a memory, but sometimes we later realize we have captured the essence of something much greater. On the best days, a camera gives us the eye of God: we see holiness.

Poet and author Diane Ackerman once wrote,

> To some extent Art is like trapping nature inside a paperweight. Suddenly a locale, or an abstract emotion, is viewable at one's leisure, falls out of flux, can be rotated and considered from different vantage points, becomes as fixed and to that extent as holy as the landscape.[3]

The camera gives us each a passkey to this artistry. As we stop and notice more images, and take more pictures, we can slow down to experience the beautiful moments of life. We can realize that our lives are art, and we are artists. We can find the little piece of artist inside of us—a piece that resembles and honors God.

Our visual sense, our ability to distinguish light from dark, green from purple, sharp angles from soft curves, is a gift. Vision allows us to connect intimately with the world around us. And vision is unique to each of us. You are the only person to "see" the world the way you do. Just like the paintings of Cezanne (who was nearsighted) or Monet (affected by cataracts), your view of the world can be a gift to those around you.

I have always been a very visual person. I am not a painter or a sculptor or a graphic designer, but I can see. I can observe and experiment. I can look for colors and shapes. And with the help of technology, I can capture them.

Images are important to me. My first memory is not one of smell or touch or sound, but of the way the sunlight fell on the door frame of our Volvo in the first moment that I held my newborn sister. Images help me get in touch with my soul. I think again of what Thomas Moore wrote:

> *The photograph empties me of agendas and worries and places me in the rare atmosphere of pure wonder. There it is that things happen, that life renews itself through a visit to the past. A photograph is liminal space, neither real nor imaginary, a middle region where the soul comes to life. To the literal mind, a photograph may look like a record of the past, but to the poetic mind it is an uncanny presencing of self and world that is pure, deep, and revealing.*[4]

As I write this book, I am four months pregnant—and overwhelmed with hopes for the little one inside me. I am in awe of the responsibility placed upon me: to nurture and love another human being. This duty excites me and scares me. But one

thing I know: I want to be good at it. I want to pass on the gifts my parents and grandparents have given me. I know our child may be serious or silly, quiet or expressive, active or mellow, artistic or verbal—or maybe a combination of all of these—and I also know there are certain values I hope to make visible within our child. I've tried to capture my vision for this on the page to the left.

God has given us the ability to perceive what *is* through our senses. But perhaps an even greater gift is our ability to imagine what *can be*—purposeful visions of what we, our lives, and the world can become. It is our privilege, and our responsibility, to nurture, shelter, and express that vision. Take your vision and make it tangible. As you scrapbook your vision, include not just what you see, but what you believe—your hopes and your values and dreams.

AN ENVISIONING EXPERIENCE

Project: To create a scrapbook journal page that makes the way you see your life visible.

The visionary is the one who brings his or her voice into the world and who refuses to edit, rehearse, perform, or hide. It is the visionary who knows that the power of creativity is aligned with authenticity.

—ANGELES ARRIEN

1. Start by closing your eyes and picturing your life.

> *What are the sights of your everyday life?*
>
> *What significant images represent what you value on a daily basis?*
>
> *What theme seems to unify your life at this time?*
>
> *What central aspect of your life would you like to explore and celebrate on your scrapbook page?*

4-1

2. What photographs do you have (or need to take) that will illustrate the way you see your life? Here are some techniques that can help you express your sense of vision:

- *Take photographs with an eye for your focal point: use a frame such as a doorway or window to draw the eye to the subject of your image. (See photo 4-1.)*

4-2

- *Lines such as the horizon or fences can do the same. (See photos 4-2 and 4-3.)*

- *Communicate movement with your photographs. Use an element in the scene (such as a path or road) to create a line. (See photo 4-4.)*

- *Or take a photograph of people in a linear arrangement. (See photo 4-5.)*

4-3

- *Take pictures of the little things at an event. Use them to expand the vision of your layout. (See photo 4-6.)*

4-4

3. Once you have chosen your photographs, consider the basic elements of your page.

• *Think about the overall visual impact of your layout. Play with geometric designs or large graphic patterns. (See layouts 4-7 and 4-8.)*

• *Or you might use one large picture to represent your journaling and theme. (See layout 4-9.)*

• *Consider what will further describe and clarify how you see your life: Additional photographs? Drawings? A title? A quotation? A word or letters?*

4-5

• *Consider how you will emphasize them: Size? Contrast? Line? Color? A combination of these?*

4. Once you have some ideas in mind, draw a quick sketch, if that helps you. Remember that it is not necessary to plan all the details of your page; just start with an intentional idea. You can

4-6

add other embellishments or support-ing images as you work. Creating is a process, and you might be surprised by what appears on the journey.

5. Begin your page. Use whatever medi-ums please you to create the page: paint, paper, stitching, stamps, markers, stickers, digital technology. If you'd like some ideas, check Appendix A for sug-gestions about accents, stamps, fonts, sewing, paint, and more. Be open to creative ideas as they come. Even though you started with a rough plan, your page will evolve as you work.

4-7

6. Include your thoughts in the form of journaling. Here are some questions to consider:

> *What do you see in the photo(s) that you may not have noticed before?*
>
> *What does your page illustrate about how you see the world?*
>
> *What does the page tell you about what is important to you?*

4-8

7. Continue working until your page reflects the way you see your world.

8. When you are satisfied, give yourself some time to reflect on these questions:

> *Where is there beauty in your life? What could you do to be more aware of it? To celebrate it? To share it?*
>
> *What is something unique about yourself that you haven't been pay-ing attention to?*
>
> *What do you want to tell those you love about what you see in them?*

4-9

How do you think God might be nudging you to use your imagination more?

How can you live out your vision in this world?

If you'd like to see how Kelly Lautenbach and I interpreted this envisioning exercise, see "I See" and "Family" on the color insert.

Going Deeper

Additional exercises to expand your vision.

> *Cherish your visions; cherish your ideals ...*
> *if you but remain true to them,*
> *your world will at last be built.*
>
> —JAMES ALLEN

✳ What do you see when you look to the future? Create a scrapbook page about your vision for the next five years.

✳ Find a photograph that is at least twenty years old. Use it in a scrapbook page that compares what you knew about yourself then to what you know now.

✳ Take a photograph of an inanimate object and use it to create a scrapbook page about someone you love. Think of this person's unique qualities that you especially value.

✳ Are you nearsighted or farsighted? How does your physical sight symbolize the way you "see" the world? Create a scrapbook page that reflects both your gifts and your limitations.

✳ Think about the invisible things in your daily life: the sound of the leaves in autumn, the smell of your baby, the feeling of family. Create a scrapbook page that makes the unseen visible.

✳ Photograph something(s) that symbolizes your faith, your values. Create a scrapbook page that describes what these symbol(s) mean to you.

A Voice along the Journey

Heather Preckel

I would have never thought I'd find my voice by simply scrapbooking; but that is what happened for me. I had always been pretty shy and just plain quiet growing up and throughout my teenage years. Reading was my escape, and I spent most of my time hidden behind the cover of a book.

I started scrapbooking as a hobby when our little girl was born, and I never expected it to become what it has today. I loved it from the second I started—the pictures, the pretty papers, the stickers, putting my heart down on my pages. It was always easier for me to write my feelings than verbalize them, so I would put my heart into each page I created so others would know what was inside my head.

My family owns a county craft store, and we added scrapbooking supplies about five years ago. I also decided to try teaching a few classes, since I had a love for it and it was pretty new to the area. It was one of those things I did before putting much thought into it, or I know I would have backed out. The thought of getting up in front of people and teaching—or just plain talking—would almost make me want to toss my cookies! But I did it, and as I stood there teaching my first class to a group of about fifteen, something broke inside of me in a good way. I was teaching and sharing something I had a love and passion for, and my nervousness went away. The sweaty palms stopped; my voice didn't shake. It was amazing! It was something I had never experienced before, and it became something I desired to do more and more.

I now travel and teach when I can and often think back to my very first class and how, had I not gotten up there, I could still be that shy quiet girl, afraid to talk in front of people. I can truly say that scrapbooking helped me find my voice—helped me find the person I was created to be, helped me overcome a big obstacle in my life, pushed me to be creative and to share that with others. I never want to take that for granted. Scrapbooking has changed and blessed my life in more ways than I would have ever expected!

5

Expression
Finding Your Voice

We are cups, constantly and quietly being filled.
The trick is, knowing how to tip ourselves over
and let the beautiful stuff out.

—RAY BRADBURY

What kinds of things do you write in an ordinary day?
  Lists? E-mails? Reminders?
When was the last time you sent a handwritten letter?
Have you ever kept a journal?
Have you ever thought about writing a book?

Even though we are surrounded by written words—advertising, magazines, newspapers, e-mail, and blogs—we rarely put our intimate thoughts and feelings into words, let alone share our written expressions with another person. To some extent, we have lost the most meaningful writing of all: personal letters. Far from the mundane written communication of our daily lives, handwritten letters are expressive, personal gifts of time and feelings.

Scrapbooking gives us the chance to write these "letters" to our friends and family. We have a safe space to pour out our hearts, to document the moments that move us, and to write love letters to the people who have shared these moments.

Many people dream of writing a book, and creating scrapbooks allows us to do just that: we publish a book for our families, creating pages where our words will last. Long after the feelings pass, our pictures and written words will live on as a tribute to the moment.

The Power of Words

Words, once they are printed,
have a life of their own.

—CAROL BURNETT

Throughout my life, books have nourished and enlightened me. They are my constant companions. At their most basic level, books are simply the words of another person preserved on paper, but they can be very powerful. Books give us insight into other people's minds and hearts and souls. They are gifts of intimacy and truth. Reading a book is like sitting down to a conversation. The author does most of the talking, but the reader's mind is engaged and active: questioning, processing, appreciating, marveling. When we finish a good book, we have a greater sense of ourselves.

Every time we read, we are breaking a code. It is so familiar to us that we don't realize it. But in reality, all words are symbols that combine thoughts and feelings into sentences, paragraphs, and chapters. They are symbols that carry extraordinary weight and power.

I've always been timid about putting words about myself on paper. I started my first real journal when I was thirteen, and I used code words and symbols to keep my dearest secrets. It was the only place where I felt I could express what I was really feeling. I could hardly bring myself to doodle in class, and I quickly crossed out any notes that I wrote to friends in the margins of my papers. I don't know what I was afraid of. Maybe the idea that if people read my truth, they would reject me. Or laugh at me. Or talk about me.

Now, journaling is an important part of my scrapbooking, but I didn't always feel this way. When I first started scrapbooking, none of my pages had words except for names, dates, and places—and the occasional quotation or poem. It took me a while to allow my words onto my scrapbook pages. At first I didn't know what to say about these beautiful memories (or I was too self-conscious to say it), so I let my photographs speak for themselves. But as the years passed and I kept on writing in my journal, those words slowly began to spill into my scrapbooks.

I remember the first time I wrote about my feelings on a scrapbook page. I was making a gift album for dear friends Amy and Scott, a couple we had met during our engagement. I had just read a new scrapbooking magazine and was eager to explore fresh ideas, so I incorporated all sorts of new-to-me embellishments, such as beads and wire and buttons. And, most important, I challenged myself to add journaling. When I gave the gift to my friends, I felt as if it had a lot more "me" in it because I had included my words. I had given them a piece of myself, not just a collection of photographs.

Soon after that, I started writing on every scrapbook page I made. I wrote something more than the facts, something about my feelings and impressions of the moment or event. Now, writing has come to be one of my favorite parts of the scrapbooking process, and I don't feel as if a page is complete unless it expresses some words from my heart.

I don't mean to imply that every moment has to be defined or embellished with words. Sometimes we can just decorate our photographs and enjoy the right-brained experience of letting images speak. Sometimes the gift of scrapbooks is that they allow us to be speechless. But I do think the intimacy of our words changes scrapbooks from a document of history to an expression of our experience. And by intimate, I don't mean words such as:

We got together on January 1, 2005, for a mini-reunion. I enjoyed taking pictures of my friends

laughing and hanging out. We ate dinner at a
Mexican restaurant and stayed up late talking.

I'm talking about something more like this:

What I keep. All of us, growing, learning ... finding
ourselves in this world in so many different ways.
Walking the paths of our lives. And reconnecting
here and there, abundant in love ... ten people who
find joy in life, who live with spirit, who find mean-
ing everywhere. This is what I keep. You. Your
smiles. Your love. The way you look at me when I
am talking. The way you look at each other. The
way you live your lives ... devoted to growth, to
helping, to giving, to God. A decade of friendships.
Laughter. The beauty of seeing you choose life part-
ners. Feeling so safe. Depth. How lucky am I to
have you in my life.

The best pages include both perspectives: details of the event (for
memory's sake), *and* the author's feelings about the experience.
When we document our experience and express our feelings in
words on a scrapbook page, we are doing more than a craft: we
are telling our story, preserving our experiences for the future.

And we are giving a glimpse of ourselves, the authors. The power of our words lives on.

The Gift of Story

*There is no agony like bearing an
untold story inside of you.*

—MAYA ANGELOU

In her book *Writing to Change the World*, Mary Pipher describes the importance of sharing our stories:

> *Stories are the most basic tool for connecting us to one another. Research shows that storytelling not only engages all the senses, it triggers activity on both the left and the right sides of the brain. Because stories elicit whole brain/whole body responses, they are far more likely than other kinds of writing to evoke strong emotions. People attend, remember, and are transformed by stories, which are meaning-filled units of ideas, the verbal equivalent of mother's milk.*
>
> *Healthy cultures pass on healthy stories from generation to generation.*[1]

By passing on stories within our families, we can help create this "healthy culture." Children (and adults, too) need to know that they are connected. We need to know we are connected to each other, to the Earth, to what has come before and what will come after. Stories help us say, "Oh, yes, I've been there, too," or empathize, "Wow, that must have been hard for you." It doesn't matter whether or not we all have the same stories. What matters is that we all have stories to tell.

So much of our culture comes at us in little bursts: glaring headlines, strips along the bottom of television screens, sound bites on the evening news. Writing our stories reminds us to slow

down and dig beneath the surface, to what really matters. When we write our stories down and share them with our children and the people we love, we give them both memories and hope.

I love watching my two-year-old godson, Ryan, as he pages through the scrapbooks his mother (and my dear friend) Amy has made. He can't read the stories yet, but he looks at the photographs and knows they tell a story about him and the people who love him. I imagine him at five, fifteen, or thirty years of age looking through these books, seeing his life story through his mother's eyes. What a gift she has given to him!

And I know I have my own unique stories to tell Ryan, too. When I create a page or mini-book about time we've spent with him and his parents, I am giving him the gift of his world through my eyes. When I create a page about our trip to the zoo, or weekend in the mountains, or walk in the park, I am letting him know that I cherish the moments we have had together. And when I write my thoughts and feelings to accompany the photographs on these pages, I am writing to remember and to celebrate our story. Like this page, with a photograph taken right before Ryan's second birthday as he and Amy played chase. I loved witnessing this mother/son moment, and documenting it.

During his years as associate editor for *Simple Scrapbooks*, Mark Zoellner has written some marvelous pieces in his "Write from the Heart" column, so I asked him if he would be willing to share some of his thoughts in this book about the importance of our stories. Here's what he wrote:

I spend my days reading the journaling of scrapbookers who make pretty pages about themselves and their loved ones. The best of these layouts employ time-tested design principles, and they may or may not make use of current embellishments that stand out among a crowded field of contenders. Good photos, courtesy of today's amazing digital cameras, complement these pages, as do vintage photographs lovingly restored.

But I mostly look at the stories. *Moms and sisters and aunties who write of their children, their parents, their pets, their partners. They journal their joys and their pain. They tell me, an absolute stranger, about a baby's first words; a fourth-grader's first goal scored; a lovely teenager who's becoming a woman; a zany boyfriend or a thoughtful husband; a wrenching career change; a mother who's facing the end of her days.*

They document their lives on a scrapbook page. This simple act is a spiritual exercise. Scrapbookers enable families—however we define that marvelous term—to see themselves as they were in time, and how they related to others. Scrapbookers, though, largely by virtue of what they write, allow their loved ones to know a bit more of how this woman felt, a little more of her interior world, the mystery and depth of this camera-wielding person who labored selflessly to nourish the people she cared for.

When we share our stories in our scrapbooks, we are not only sharing our feelings about our lives, but we are also connecting with those who will view our pages. Our stories ground us and connect us. They help us experience ourselves as human by leading us through our emotions, from joy to grief. They not only help us to know ourselves, but they also remind us of our universal experience.

The Journey of Writing

The act of writing is the act
of discovering what you believe.

—DAVID HARE

Writing is an action that helps define us. In searching for the right words, we search for meaning inside ourselves. We listen to the voice within that speaks our truth. I think this is why Julia Cameron includes writing as a basic step in her book *The Artist's Way.* To become an artist, we need to know who we are ... even if all we can get is a little glimpse. Writing makes our souls visible, both to ourselves and to others.

The writing process, however, is not always easy. Deep, exploratory writing can be exhausting. There are times I'd rather sit and "watch" than do the work of sorting, analyzing, or reflecting. But it's the difference between taking in a beautiful mountain vista from a roadside pull-off and hiking the Appalachian Trail—covered with sweaty dirt, smelling the earth, feeling the wind. *Not writing* is easy. But in not writing, we miss the journey.

Nor is the writing process always beautiful. When we search for our truth, we may find ugliness, too. We see our insecurities and fears. We see the darkness. But when we make the darkness visible, we can stop carrying it around inside us.

One of the things that John and I continually see in our work with our girls is how much they are overcome by darkness. They are filled with anger. They are burdened by sadness. Misplaced frustration almost always accompanies them. But we believe, and we trust, that they can be stronger than all of it. We know the darkness will not go away. But it can be released.

So we teach them to write about their journey. We teach them that writing releases darkness. That writing is a way to empty themselves to clear space for potential, to make room for the presence of hope and light. As they write, shadows can pour onto the page, flowing through the arm and the pen. Their words can hold the tension so they no longer have to. If I could instill in them one practice, it would be this: If there is darkness, write. If there is only silence, write. For there is something to be heard. Write privately, for the searching words are not to be interpreted by any other hearts. Write through the questions and uncertainty. Write until your shoulders rest and your face relaxes. Write to find peace. Write to find home. Write until you reach the other side of pain and anger. Then, and only then, write to share. Share the darkness, but share the celebrations and beauty as well. Whatever you write, your words will capture your truth in your own words. Your words will *be* a gift—and *bring* a gift, the gift of healing.

A friend once told me that one of my scrapbook pages really helped her in her relationship with her husband. I had created a page with several silly pictures of my husband, John, and included journaling about how his goofiness was a gift to me and to our girls. I wrote:

Hey buddy, this is supposed to be a serious photo shoot! It's not even for you, it's for our girls. Come on, just hold still and smile nicely so I can check the lighting.

Oh well. My playful husband brings my attempts at serious art back to reality. And I am so grateful for his goofiness. Just when I am getting too serious, he reminds me that life is joyous. I cannot count the number of times that one of our girls has made some semi-grumpy remark to which I am about to

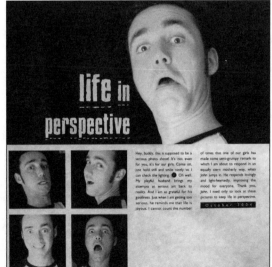

*respond in an equally stern motherly way, when
John jumps in. He responds lovingly and lightheart-
edly, improving the mood for everyone. Thank you,
John. I need only to look at these pictures to keep
life in perspective.*

My friend told me that when she read the journaling on the page,
it made her think of her husband and his gifts in a new way. It
quelled some of her annoyance and gave her a new perspective.
It gave her hope. And it does the same for me, whenever I revisit
the page.

On many levels, the practice of writing in our scrapbooks is
a healing endeavor. As Anne Lamott tells us in *Bird by Bird*:

*Your anger and damage and grief are the way to the
truth. We don't have much truth to express unless we
have gone into those rooms and closets and woods
and abysses that we were told not to go in to. When
we have gone in and looked around for a long while,
just breathing and finally taking it in—then we will
be able to speak in our own voice and to stay in the
present moment. And that moment is home.[2]*

Having said all this, I have to confess: writing is sometimes
the hardest part of the scrapbooking page. It is not taking pictures. It is not selecting pretty paper. It is delving, probing,
asking:

What really matters?

What does this mean?

How can I tell this story?

Writing is a *doing* activity—full engagement of the mind, the
hand, and, mostly, the sense of observation. It is a foil to the art
of photography, where we merely observe without qualifying or
describing. But the juxtaposition of words and images speaks
volumes about our essential selves.

During a particularly lonely period of my life, I was consumed by scrapbooking. It was my companion when people
couldn't be. Since I lived at least two hours from my dearest

friends and family, I saw them off and on throughout the year, but I did not have the day-to-day contact I really wanted. I found it particularly difficult to be far away from my girlfriends and female family members.

One day I gathered photographs of the twelve most significant women in my life. I saw them all together in my mind, almost holding hands in a protective circle around me. I thought of my grandmothers and aunts and friends and all the gifts they have brought into my life and the ways they've shaped me. And I started to write.

I poured out my words, and my heart, to express the profound ways these women affected me, every day, even when they were miles away. I documented how Grandma Corinne's quiet gentleness and the memory of her soft hands still soothe me, even after her death. I wrote about my sister Sarah's steady presence. I recorded my friend Tammy's loyalty to both self and family that inspires me to grow. On and on I wrote, celebrating the gifts these twelve women have brought to my life. And I cried through my writing, overcome with gratitude and warmth.

Days later I combined my writing and the photographs, along with a few embellishments and a symbolic picture of community. My layout was complete. I e-mailed a copy of it to my twelve companions, who responded with tears and letters of gratitude. And when the loneliness creeps back, I remember. I am not alone.

Maybe you are hesitant to personalize a beautifully laid-out scrapbook page with writing. Although photographs are a huge component of scrapbooks—and they are a great gift—they do not have the intimacy of our words. Our words share what is true for us. Our words tell our journey. Our words are love letters to the people who matter, who care about us. Our words can help us heal.

AN EXPRESSIVE EXPERIENCE

Project: To create a scrapbook journal page that explores the richness and depth of your words.

Writing, I think, is not apart from living. Writing is a kind of double living. The writer experiences everything twice. Once in reality and once in the mirror which waits always before or behind.

—Catherine Drinker Bowen

1. Rather than starting with a photograph, start by finding something meaningful that you have written—an e-mail, a poem, an excerpt from your journal, a letter, even something mundane like a list. The point is to use something unique to you and your experience—your voice.

2. Read your words slowly and carefully. Then consider how you might want to illustrate your words. Here are some possibilities:

   • *Write your words by hand in straight lines. (See layout 5-1.)*

   • *Write your words in shapes, such as swirls or circles. (See layout 5-2.)*

5-1

5-2

- Format the text on a computer and print it out in various fonts (see Appendix A for information on fonts). (See layout 5-3.)

- Use stamps, stickers, or rub-ons. For example, layout 5-4 includes computer fonts for the word *October* and for journaling, stickers for the *S* and the *M*, and rub-ons.

- Hide journaling (handwritten or typed) behind an element on your page. Put it inside a decorated envelope, create a pull-out feature by attaching ribbon to cardstock, or fashion a paper "hinge" on a photograph so that it can be lifted to view the journaling underneath. In layout 5-5, from my Advent scrapbook journal, the photograph on the left side is hinged. The tab below the date lifts the photograph to expose journaling about the story of the wrapping paper I used during the season.

- Use manufacturer's premade stickers or labels. For example, layout 5-6 includes a premade initial stencil (*A*) with descriptive

5-3

5-4

words, a rub-on with the word *confidence,* and a sticker with the word *you.* I added *celebrating* with an image-editing program.

3. Whatever materials you use, play as you create. Let the words take shape on the page. Create a title if you want. Use photographs or drawings to help, if you desire. Emphasize them with size, contrast, line, and color. Remember three things as you build your page:

- *Emphasize your main idea: the focal point.*
- *Balance shapes, colors, and textures and keep proportion in mind.*
- *Include a sense of movement with horizontal or curved elements, repetition, and the visual triangle.*

5-5

4. Add supportive journaling to your page. Consider these questions:

> *When did you write these words?*
>
> *What did they mean to you then?*
>
> *What do they mean to you now?*
>
> *What do these words tell you about yourself?*

5. Continue working until you feel your page communicates your thoughts and feelings and visually satisfies you.

6. Give yourself some time to reflect on your page with these questions:

5-6

> *Where are words important in my life right now?*
>
> *Where would I like to be saying more?*
>
> *Who is listening to my words? Who else would I like to hear them?*
>
> *Is there anything in my life I would like to put into writing?*
>
> *Is there anyone to whom I would like to tell my story? What is important for that person to know?*

If you'd like to see how Danielle Catalano-Titus and I interpreted this expressive exercise, see "Lost and Found" and "This Sacred Place" on the color insert.

Going Deeper

Additional exercises in written expression.

> *Don't try to figure out what other people want to
> hear from you; figure out what you have to say.
> It's the one and only thing you have to offer.*
>
> —BARBARA KINGSOLVER

✳ Create a scrapbook page about an important event. In
addition to photographs, explore in writing the five Ws of
the event: who, what, when, where, and why. Add words
that emphasize the small details, such as the sense of taste
or smell you associate with the photographs.

✳ Make a scrapbook page about your name. Explore in
words your response to these questions: How did you get
your name? How do you feel about it?

✳ Free-write about a memory. Record your thoughts and
feelings without censure or judgment. After you have written them, go back and select pieces of your writing as the
basis for a scrapbook page.

✳ Think of a memory. List the nouns and verbs you associate
with it. List the adjectives and adverbs. (Use a thesaurus if
you want to expand your list or express something differently.) Then select some of these words as the beginning
point for a scrapbook page.

✳ Think of yourself as the author of your future. Write about
your hopes and dreams. Then create a scrapbook page
that builds on these words, as a symbol of your potential.

Notes

A Voice along the Journey

SHARYN TORMANEN

I'm not sure if I would say that scrapbooking has awakened me. Rather, scrapbooking has helped me clarify the things in this life that are the most important. To be honest, it's my six-year-old who really taught me this lesson. It's not uncommon to spy her sitting in the corner recliner with a huge stack of albums beside her. As she flips through, page by page, it's not the well-embellished documentation of her first day of school, or the page celebrating her fifth birthday party, that elicit comments. Rather, it's the pages that share stories of our every day, the stories behind our family jokes, the stories of our traditions. It's the small moments we share together that bring forth her "Oh, I remember that time!" exclamations of joy.

And you know what? I lied. Scrapbooking *did* awaken me. It's thinking of my daughter and recalling her comments that so often reminds me to set aside those dirty dishes and let the laundry pile up to make the time to create more everyday moments. Because those are the opportunities that will too soon be gone if I don't grasp them now.

6

Awakening Coming Alive

Don't ask yourself what the world needs;
ask yourself what makes you come alive.
And then go and do that. Because what the world
needs is people who have come alive.

—HAROLD WHITMAN

What gives your life variety?
What stimulates you?
What surprises you?
What makes you feel alive?

I think one of the reasons many of us are drawn to scrapbooking is that it makes us feel alive. Suddenly, we start noticing details we had previously overlooked. As we combine life examination with creative expression, we have a new appreciation for life's gifts. In addition, many of us have not been encouraged as adults to be creative, so the chance to express ourselves artistically is freeing. Scrapbooking offers endless opportunities for play and experimentation, and helps us fight stagnation by teaching us new ways to see and experience our lives.

Appreciating Variety

There is no blue without yellow and without orange.

—VINCENT VAN GOGH

What teaches us diversity better than color? Color is what we see when a surface reflects certain wavelengths of light. We tend to simplify colors to the seven colors of the rainbow (red, orange, yellow, green, blue, indigo, violet), plus black and white. But the magic is that each color has seemingly countless shades. Think of the green of an elm tree in comparison to the green of the grass or the green of a mountain lake. Even though they are each "green," they have endless nuances that distinguish them from each other. A color can be perfectly green or perfectly blue, but it is never The Perfect Color. One color cannot compete with other colors. It can only be itself.

We tend to think of colors as warm or cool. Warm colors, such as red, orange, and yellow, convey energy and emotion. Cool colors, such as blue and some shades of green, have a calming effect. Some colors have both cool and warm tones, such as purple and turquoise. These colors hold energy, a push/pull tension that keeps us alert and lively. (Remember this the next time you are choosing a color for a scrapbook page: the unpredictable mixes of warm and cool, of primary and secondary, maintain productive tension in a layout and help it come alive.)

Scrapbooking brings us in touch with color in intimate ways. Suddenly, we are making choices about colors: Which colors appeal to the eye? Which combinations are pleasing? Which combinations create energy? Which combinations create serenity?

For the first couple of years that I scrapbooked, I used only plum, forest green, and navy paper on my pages, regardless of the colors or moods of the photographs. But after I started reading scrapbooking magazines, colors leaped onto my pages and I began using them in mindful ways. Two early pages stand out in my memory.

One includes photographs from a small garden that we visited near Acadia National Park in Maine. Inspired by the yellow and pink flowers and warm sunlight in the photographs, I used a light pink background and accented it with deeper pink, warm greens, and bright yellows. Pink chalking and yellow eyelets added texture and dimension. The page is full of both energy and softness.

The second reflects the rugged and windswept geography of eastern Nebraska. I used a medium-orange back-

6-1. "I See" by Cory Richardson-Lauve (see color insert).

ground to contrast with the blue sky in the focal point picture. I added words in a deeper orange and used deep orange fiber and ivory mesh for texture. The orange is brilliant and breathtaking—just like the composition of earth and sky in the Midwest.

Awakening to colors on these early pages has led to a love of color on all my pages. For example, on layout 6-1, I was drawn to the brilliant pink of the flower in my focal point photograph. I enhanced the other hues in the photograph (green and yellow) with image-editing software, and I chose a turquoise background that would not overwhelm the other photographs.

On layout 6-2, the blues in the photographs stood out to me. I arranged the photographs with blue in them in a visual triangle to maintain the balance and movement of the layout, and I added a rose background to complement the blue.

Notice how these two layouts, though they use similar colors, convey different moods. "I See" is more energetic, while "Remember" is more restful and contemplative. For me, each layout is a chance to create a unique palette—a chance to experiment and play.

6-2. "Remember" by Cory Richardson-Lauve
(see color insert).

Certain colors make us sigh and certain colors invigorate us. This is also true of our relationships and our surroundings. We have friends who bring out the yellow in us and friends who find the turquoise. There are blue days and red days and peach days. One of the most powerful lessons of color is that it reminds us not to turn our lives—or our scrapbooks—into a game of hierarchy, but to embrace variety. Just as we need different colors for different purposes on our pages, so, too, do we need a variety of people to fulfill different roles in our lives.

As you scrapbook, give yourself permission to play with color, experimenting with shades you wouldn't ordinarily use or put next to each other. As you let yourself appreciate the variety of color, allow it take you in new directions—in your scrapbook and in your life.

Stimulating Your Creativity

Creativity is a type of learning process where the teacher and pupil are located in the same individual.

—ARTHUR KOESTLER

One of the gifts of scrapbooking is the way it awakens creativity. I wrote about it in my journal one night:

> *It is 12:52 a.m. and I am supposed to be asleep. My mind flutters with book ideas and page*

concepts. The contest deadline is a month away, and I am challenged once again beyond my natural rhythms. It almost hurt to keep my eyes closed in bed, as I listened to John's even breathing and willed myself to sleep. An hour later I am still awake, and have decided not to fight it. I've read about people who cannot sleep. Minds awash with ideas, they do not fight for sleep but instead revel in the quiet of darkness. They paint and write poetry and sculpt, and I imagine more than a few of them scrapbook. Me, I usually just try to read until sleep overcomes me, but tonight there are too many thoughts. I have to make visible the jumble of ideas and energy inside me.

Something inside us longs for artistic expression, for a way to make our ideas visible. But sometimes we get this confused with a need for entertainment, as Thomas Moore notes in *Handbook for the Soul*, "We don't need to be entertained nearly as much as we need to give the soul the images it craves."[1] Movies and thirty-minute sitcoms distract us and occupy us, but they do not feed us. Like lemon meringue pie, they are pleasurable and sweet, but they do not nourish us. In fact, too much of them might give us a headache. But creative pursuits that involve soul-filled images, such as scrapbooking, satisfy us like a well-balanced meal (followed by dessert!), feeding our need for creative expression.

At times, though, we get the pleasure of creativity mixed up with the pleasure of pleasing others. I confess: I sometimes find myself looking for the admiration of my peers when I scrapbook. I am not just sharing my joy. I am looking for affirmation and approval and, if I'm lucky, a chance to impress someone. And though I might get some of this, I never seem to get enough. There is never enough praise to fill me. When I recognize this emptiness in me, it propels me back to what matters. Instead of ceasing to create, I create again, only this time I return to make something uniquely me.

You might be saying, "Maybe that works for you; you're the 'creative' type. But I don't know where to start." If you find yourself stuck, look around you for creative stimulation. The fire of creativity needs the energy of ideas. Here are some ways to spark your creativity:

- Look at magazines or online galleries for inspiration.
- Learn a new scrapbooking technique (digital or traditional).
- Take a walk in your neighborhood and bring your camera. Take pictures of things you haven't noticed before.
- Use a color that you haven't used on your last ten pages.
- Do a supply exchange with a friend and try out some new products.
- Take a break. Enjoy art in another form, such as music, paintings, or gardens, so you can come back to scrapbooking from a new standpoint.
- Change the focal point of your page. If it is usually a photograph, for example, use lyrics or journaling instead.

Each time you return to the process of creating, you'll find not external praise, but internal joy. Not admiration, but pleasure. Not impressing others, but growing closer to the people in your life. Think of your creative process not as a challenge but as a celebration of your ability to co-create with God.

Welcoming Surprises

The moments of happiness we enjoy take us
by surprise. It is not that we seize them,
but that they seize us.

—ASHLEY MONTAGU

When I first started scrapbooking, I was swept away. It became a passion, I think, because it offered me surprise. As I discovered the artist within and found new ways of expression, scrapbooking introduced me to new joys.

But now, after a decade of scrapbooking and two years of being engulfed in the industry, I am not so surprised anymore. At this point, scrapbooking is more like a time-tested relationship; it does not offer new vistas around every corner. Instead, it surprises me in deeper, more meaningful ways.

I am surprised by the way scrapbooking has changed the way I see the world. I look at moments and connections dif-

6-3. "This Changes Me" by Cory Richardson-Lauve (see color insert).

ferently. Scrapbooking substance is everywhere. Color swatches at a furniture store inspire me with their juxtaposition. Each tiny moment—such as a father and son walking into a restaurant together, laughing—suddenly captures the truth of love and connection. A photograph shines with the essence of a dear friend.

The *process* of scrapbooking also continues to surprise me: the way a page unfolds differently every time, the fact that we, in our human form, can imitate the profound variety of God's creation. I love the experience of trimming a piece of paper and then, accidentally, turning it a quarter-turn. Suddenly the layout moves in new directions, and I am propelled forward by possibilities.

When I created layout 6-3, about my relationship with John, the process took me on a journey. I started with just a photograph that I imprinted with the word *this*, and then I played with different cardstocks and patterned paper. I realized I had letters that would work with the size of the page. I sought balance by using white paint on stamps to create patterns on the paper. A bit of stitching added texture. The process relaxed me and carried me. The surprises in the process (such as finding the faint white sticker letters I used at the top of the page) brought me joy.

The way colors blend and contrast in endless ways is another of scrapbooking's ongoing surprises. Colors can be combined in so many unpredictable ways! I think of what Pablo Picasso once said: "Why do two colors, put one next to the other, sing? Can one really explain this?" Scrapbooking celebrates this wonderful surprise.

I am also continually surprised by the work of other artists. It amazes me, really, the infinite ways people can combine colors, images, and words. Today I saw a relatively simple page completed by another artist: one photograph, one sheet of pattern paper, some stamps, handwritten journaling, a white background. The asymmetry of the background complemented the clean lines of the page, which contrasted with the depth of multiple layers of stamped images. The whole image was unified by a frame of handwritten journaling. Simple—yet surprising. I love being surprised and inspired by another scrapbooker's vision.

If you're the kind of person who likes things to go as planned, scrapbooking can help you embrace the surprises of life. One of the gifts of scrapbooking is the pleasure of the unknown. As you work, let the process flow. Let yourself imagine trying things a different way: "What would happen if I turned that picture sideways and then overlapped it with a word?" "How might that new technique I read about liven up my page?"

Perhaps the best thing about surprises—in scrapbooking and in life—is the unexpected joy they can bring. Who would have guessed that deep coral could make cyan sing? Who would have thought that job you volunteered to do would have turned out so interesting? Who would have guessed that you would have met someone so in tune with your interests at that party? When we are open to the surprises life brings, we find that we have the capacity to still be seized by wonder.

The Art of Everyday

*The real voyage of discovery consists not in seeing
new landscapes but in having new eyes.*

—MARCEL PROUST

Even with all its variety and surprise, life can be tedious and repetitive. We seem to live the same days over and over as we care for our families and ourselves. The shapes of our lives seem to be the same color—or even a variety of colors, but they blend to a dull gray. This repetition can lead to boredom or even depression. But there are lessons to learn from this boredom.

I recently read an article about finding the Zen in surfing.[2] We tend to look for the peaks in our lives—the great waves that catapult us forward, give us a ride, exhilarate us. But the "flats" matter, too: the in-between times, the waiting, and the half-formed waves that trick us into paddling swiftly with our hands, only to disappoint us as they diminish. Often we swing hard to one side or the other, either searching only for the perfect waves or eschewing all, certain that we only learn through suffering and detachment.

Part of the art of our lives is its everydayness. Every day we see the same faces and surroundings. We see the same colors presented to us over and over again in our living rooms and on our dinner plates. This repetition is the substance of our lives.

One of my favorite albums contains a page for every day of a single month. Each day I took a picture of something that struck me: the colorful binders that hold the files of the girls that we work with, the makeup I wear on a daily basis, a pie my husband made, my flip-flops lying on the sand at the beach, a spring flower pushing up through the mulch. Nothing exceptional—no exotic vacations or newborn babies—but this album is full of color and stories, and (probably more than any of my other albums) gives the best picture of my life and the gifts that it holds. It celebrates the everyday—the quiet times and the repetition of life.

Sometimes it can be a relief to sink into quiet and repetition, to let creativity and growth rest. The lulls in scrapbooking, I am convinced, are healthy and rejuvenating. Sometimes I just want to be in this moment, quiet and still and unproductive. I want to let the day slip away without preservation or notice. I want to drink this coffee and pet the cat, call my mom, and have dinner with my husband. I want to feel the soft breeze on my suntanned shoulders and stop trying to figure out a way to photograph it. I want to stop watching people look at the photographs I take, waiting for them to say, "Ah, I see the light you captured here," or "Yes, you've portrayed Maria perfectly." I want to just *be* in this world, accepting my own (sometimes unproductive) life.

We all have these days. The secret is to rest in the quiet and trust that, in time, you will once again capture a photograph that will inspire you to tell a story or feeling; that you will see a color in a photograph that calls out for a scrapbook page; that you will see something in the world differently and feel the urge to express it in images and words. And most of all, have faith that the spirit and energy of creativity will return.

A CREATIVE EXPERIENCE

Project: To create a page that explores the variety of color in your life.

> One of the great exercises you can do is to stop and
> acknowledge the colors around you....
> If you're constantly distracting yourself, then you're
> never really experiencing anything fully.
> It can cause you to feel like you have no center,
> like nothing is grounding you.
>
> —SHERYL CROW

1. Start by considering these questions:

What colors surround you?

What colors do you wear most often?

How would you describe the people around you in terms of color?

How do colors enrich you?

2. Select some photographs or drawings that incorporate these colors. Then journal your response to this question:

What do these different colors mean to you?

6-4. "Life" by Cory Richardson-Lauve (see color insert).

3. Design a page that includes words from your journaling. As you create your page, use images, shapes, and textures that represent how you include these colors in your life.

4. Give special thought to the order and vibrancy of your colors as you place them on the page.

   Layout 6-4 is a page I created doing this exercise: I followed the traditional rainbow order of colors in a circular pattern and included dozens of photographs that represent the presence of color in my life.

   Layout 6-5 is Jessie Baldwin's interpretation of this exercise. Her colors appear in a surprising sequence in a linear design, with a stitched outline of her hand that personalizes it.

5. Be open to creative ideas using color, as they come. Even if you started with a rough plan, your page will evolve as you work. Continue working until you

6-5. "Living Color/Shades of Grey" by Jessie Baldwin (see color insert).

feel your page communicates your thoughts and feelings and visually pleases you.

6. Spend some time reflecting on your page and ask yourself this question:

Are there any colors missing from your life?

Going Deeper

Additional exercises in awakening your creativity.

It is an extraordinary and beautiful thing that God, in creation, uses precisely the same tools and rules as the artist ... the beauty of matter; the reality of things; the discoveries of the senses, all five of them.

—MADELEINE L'ENGLE

6-6. See the color insert for Danielle's monochromatic layout "Lost and Found." Note that she added a touch of yellow and some black to ground the layout. But the domination of the shades of pink creates a monochromatic color scheme and captures the eye.

✳ Study the color wheel. A basic understanding of color will help you become more expressive. Use a color wheel to help you understand the nature of colors (you can view one at http://www.colormatters.com/colortheory.html).

✳ There are three primary colors: red, blue, and yellow. These colors combine with each other to create the secondary colors: green, orange, and purple. The secondary colors combine with their adjoining primary colors to create tertiary (or intermediate) colors, such as red-orange and turquoise. Once you have an awareness of colors, you can begin to understand how they interact with each other.

✳ Create a layout with a monochromatic color scheme (different shades of the same hue). (See layout 6-6.)

✳ Create a layout using analogous tones (colors next to each other on the color wheel). (See layout 6-7.)

✳ Create a layout using colors that are opposite each other on the color wheel (complementary colors). This creates energy and contrast—which is why you will often see complementary colors on the jerseys of athletic teams, such as orange and blue, or purple and yellow. (See layout 6-8.)

✳ Create a layout using three colors equidistant from each other on the color wheel (triadic colors) for a layout that is both harmonious and energizing. (See layout 6-9.)

✳ Create a well-balanced layout by being aware of how colors interact. (See layout 6-10.)

✳ Create a mini-book (small scrapbook focused on just one subject). Designate one color for each page. In nature, find an example of the essence of that color (think fruit, flowers, etc.) and create a page about it. Look closely at the design and proportion of each natural object or scene you choose and build on this in your page.

6-7. See the color insert for my layout "This Is Love" using green and blue. Note how analogous colors create a serene, calm feeling.

6-8. See the color insert for my layout "Balance" using complementary colors. Note how the blue/green background makes a strong contrast to the red/orange stripe.

6-9. See the color insert for Ursula's layout "Sharing a Childhood." Note how Ursula used muted shades of red, blue, and yellow to create a sophisticated layout.

6-10. See the color insert for Barb's layout "Precious" as an example of how to use many colors on a layout. Barb scattered the colors throughout her layout, creating a balanced page. She also used different amounts of the colors—more red and yellow, less purple and green—to add variety and surprise. Using varying amounts of color will help keep your page balanced and interesting.

❋ Document the everyday parts of your life on a scrapbook page: the contents of your pantry, the route you drive every day, your dishes and silverware, your daily routine, the books your child loves to have read to her over and over again, the most frequently cooked meals in your home, the colors of your living room.

❋ Create a scrapbook page using a new technique that you haven't tried before. Browse online galleries to let other scrapbook artists inspire you. Don't try for a "perfect page," but rather be open to the "what ifs."

Notes ⎯⎯⎯⎯⎯

A Voice along the Journey

CATHY PASCUAL

Hi, my name is Cathy. I am a shy person.

For most of my life, shyness has been my identity. The one thing that defines me. It has shaped my personality. It has shaped my relationships. It has shaped my career decisions.

Shyness has prevented me from pursuing personal interests, such as tennis (need to find a partner) and journalism (need to interview people). It is my biggest obstacle in life. It is something I've been trying to overcome for years.

Enter scrapbooking.

When I discovered this soul-satisfying, creativity-boosting hobby, I found a community who shared my interests. I began to attend crops and conventions. I've been published in magazines and even won a few contests. I've made new friends (both online and in person).

Scrapbooking nourishes a part of me that had previously been stifled. A part of me that needed an outlet for my photography, my art, my words, my story.

Now I can proudly say: Hi, my name is Cathy. I am a scrapbooker.

7

Celebration
Knowing Your True Self

People travel to wonder at the height of the mountains, at the huge waves of the seas, at the long course of the rivers, at the vast compass of the ocean, at the circular motion of the stars, and yet they pass by themselves without wondering.

—St. Augustine

Where are you successful?
What gives you energy?
When do you feel at home?
What do you really want?
How do you experience God?

In his book *Communion with God*, Neale Donald Walsh writes, "Every act is an act of self-definition."[1] I think this is especially true in every act of creativity—including every scrapbook page we create out of scraps, images, and our imaginations.

Every choice—which photographs to use, where to start, which colors will work, knowing when a page is finished, and everything in between—is a self-defining experience. Do you stick to primary colors? Notice what's happening in your life that leads to a childlike, simple, open feeling. Are you attracted by swirling, curving shapes? Maybe you are seeking a feeling of fluidity, a desire to avoid hard edges, a need to cradle softness.

Scrapbooking can take you on a journey. Not just a journey of shopping and assembling, but a journey of self-discovery and connecting—with your inner self and with God.

Listening to Yourself

Our deepest wishes are whispers of our authentic selves. We must learn to respect them. We must learn to listen.

—SARAH BAN BREATHNACH

The idea of "finding yourself" is such a cliché that I cringe to write about it. But, like most clichés, there is truth in it. Sometimes we are the greatest mystery to ourselves, which is a paradox since we spend our entire life in this body, with this soul. But it is easy to be externally focused—"Who needs my attention?" "What do I need to do?"—instead of listening to the voice in us that is saying, "This is what I want. This is what I need."

Scrapbooking offers us a way to listen, to hear ourselves. First of all, it quiets the other noises. The laundry that's waiting, the car that needs repair, the phone calls that need to be returned, tomorrow's schedule—all the routines of life become background, and the page in front of us becomes the focus. In the quiet we have a chance to listen for what really matters to us in the privacy of our thoughts and feelings, to listen for our heart's voice.

Often the best way to start a scrapbook page is to stop and listen, just for a moment. What do the photos in front of you tell you? Listen for their message. What did you capture with your camera? A sense of growth? Connections among your family? The spirit of childhood? The breathlessness of early love? The beauty of God's creation?

Then listen for what resonates within you. A particular feeling? A wish? A hope? An idea? As you look through papers, arrange photos, add design elements, and rearrange, keep listening every step of the way. Respond to what calls uniquely to you.

I remember a time I created a layout as a biography page for a website. I began by gathering photographs of me in the roles that help make me who I am. I arranged them on a digital page and experimented with fonts and layouts. Then, I listened. What else did the page need to really communicate "me"? I added a bouquet of flowers, a row of doodles, frames around certain photographs, and, most important, a background sprinkled with the word *happy*. My life is rich and full and joyous, and I wanted a page to communicate that mood.

There used to be an advertisement for diamond rings that peppered women's magazines. Its slogan read, "Women of the world, raise your right hand." The message was that a woman needs a diamond that *she*—not her fiancé—chooses, a diamond that symbolizes who she is. Although I'm not a diamond girl, there is truth in making choices that symbolize us. Scrapbooking gives us a space to "raise our right hands," to show what speaks to us and what we value. Whether you create a page about yourself or about other people, scrapbooking is an opportunity to use colors and shapes and textures that communicate "you."

Defining Yourself

The privilege of a lifetime is being who you are.

—Joseph Campbell

I used to enjoy those simplistic and fun self-defining quizzes often found in women's magazines. I am still fascinated by personality inventories such as Myers-Briggs and the Enneagram. But I also think they reduce us by attempting to fit us into neat categories.

None of us fits neatly.

One of my dearest friends, Melissa, went through a period of time in her twenties when she did not shave her legs. She kept her shapely runner's legs hairy for two summers for reasons of convenience and principle. But during that time, she continued to apply lipstick with the same devotion she had for all the years I had known her. And it was beautiful, this juxtaposition of burliness and glamour. It was uniquely her, endearing and memorable. Any quiz about her life would have omitted this tiny but so defining detail about her.

One of the reasons I love scrapbooking is that it puts us in touch with these minute details. In each decision we make about what to put on a page, we are paying attention to what is unique about us. We are choosing what represents our vision and our experience. We are choosing what to show the world. Even if the page is not about us, we are still the person presenting it. We are making a part of ourselves visible.

Recently, I was flipping through images of my scrapbook pages on my computer screen. I was filled with delight and pleasure, not because the layouts are particularly outstanding, but because they are *mine*. They are the product of my hands and my vision. They capture in the tiniest space the hugeness of my love and joy in this world. They are the details of my life made visible.

Recently, I was looking at a page about a reunion with my grandparents. I felt grateful that they are *my* grandparents. They

are so beautiful to me. And I recognize pieces of myself in them: I share their Louisiana heritage, commitment to family, and strong faith.

Sometimes I think of scrapbooks as pieces of a giant puzzle: if I could fit them all together, I could see "me." They identify who is important to me, what experiences have shaped me, how I feel. All I have to do is *look* at a page, and I can feel the emotions I was experiencing at the time. I recently revisited a page I created about a trip to Cancun, and immediately felt both the serenity and the energy of that time in the blue and green and yellow of the page.

Creating a page about a recent trip to the mountains or a visit with grandparents or a memory from childhood is not about living in the past and playing with paper. It is about naming what is important to you, defining who you are.

Many scrapbookers keep an inspiration journal—a place to collect all the bits and pieces that resonate with them, such as layouts torn from magazines, swatches of fabric, and samples of inspiring color combinations. This is a great place to start. As you collect what is meaningful to you, you begin to make visible the shapes and colors of your life.

Accepting and Celebrating Yourself

I think when I can get to that place of self-acceptance and a sense of calm assurance in who I genuinely am, if I can believe in who I am, what I need, what I deserve and what I must express, then I can let go of the struggle of self-acceptance based on their approval of my beauty, boobs, thighs, or sketchbooks. I will dare to do just what I do. Be just what I am. And dance whenever I want to.

—SABRINA WARD HARRISON

If you are anything like me, you carry around a bit of competitiveness. (If you do not, please write me and tell me what that is like.) I always want to be prettier, better, more interesting, more talented. It makes me tired. It distracts me from what really matters.

Sometimes I can get past it, and yet it is always something I have to work on. In a recent scrapbooking contest, I found myself paralyzed by competition. The calls were going out to the winners, and I could not stay away from the scrapbooking message boards. Anonymous winners would post their success, and the rest of us would scramble to see how many calls were left, which non-anonymous people were absent (possible winners?), and hold our breath to wait for the phone to ring. I hated it. But I could not stop. I wanted to win. I wanted to be the best. I wanted nothing short of perfection.

It wasn't until close to dusk, when I finally left the house to take a walk, that I could let go. It was early March and spring was on its way, but the trees were still bare and brown. As I began to pay attention to the details around me, I saw the underside of tree branches reaching toward the deep blue sky, which was tinted with orange and pink. It was stark and breathtaking and simple.

What if, at his moment, I let myself believe that everything in my life is perfect? Not flawless or unchangable or done, but just perfect for this moment. Perfectly flawed, perfectly ready for change, perfectly undone. How open would that make me? What peace would I experience?

With all that is happening in my life this busy season...baking, shopping, working, planning and hoping for this book, visiting family and friends...maybe this should be my prayer:

accept the perfection *of today*

I thought about the Creator and the process of creation. I thought about how different those trees would look in just a month, covered with the young green leaves of early spring. And how different they would look just months after that, tinted with the red of autumn. Each season offers its own gifts of life and beauty, and creation is dependent on the unique contribution of each distinctive element.

In the same vein, God creates each of us to be perfectly unique and quirky. God doesn't mean for us to be cuter or richer or more artistic or bookish or athletic. God intends us each to be *ourselves*—late winter, early spring, deep autumn. Bare branches, green sprigs, tinted leaves, and all.

Unfortunately, our society teaches us to idolize perfection: the perfect home, the perfect skin, the perfect family. There is this idea that it can all be achieved—especially if we have enough money. But this is a false promise. Perfection does not exist in this world; it is a myth we have manufactured. The reality is that all of it—from the style of our scrapbook pages to the way we live our lives to the glorious quirks of nature—is an expression of the uniqueness of God's creation.

I think that one of the best things about scrapbooking is that it gives us a place to let go of perfection and celebrate uniqueness. There is no "right" or "wrong" choice, no perfect color or paper or design—only what fits the page we have in mind. When I created the page above as an entry in my Christmas journal, I started with the freedom of journaling. As I created a page around my words, I tried to let go of my need for perfect placement, color choice, and design. I even let a typing error remain, resisting the urge to correct and reprint the page. Creating this layout evolved into an experience of accepting and celebrating the day.

Scrapbooking provides a space of freedom to choose what we want, the way we want, without worrying about offending or compromising, without winning or losing, without being the "best" or "perfect." Each choice is a discovery, another piece of knowledge about ourselves made visible. But here's the catch: the inevitable result of self-knowledge is realizing that we are not perfect. This is difficult, as Oriah Mountain Dreamer so eloquently writes:

> *It's hard to believe that I can be enough as I am. I want to be more—more compassionate, more present, more conscious and aware, more loved and loving, more intimate with myself and the world. I want to know how to be different—better—than I am. Even though I have failed to consistently live my deepest desires and am exhausted by the endless effort to become who I think I will have to be to live those desires, I resist letting go of the trying. I trust my ability to work hard. I have no experience with or faith in my ability to simply be.*[2]

The secret to *knowing* ourselves is *being* ourselves. Yet being ourselves may be one of the hardest things we do every day. It may also be the most important: it connects us with each other; it connects us with our Creator.

Each time I create a scrapbook page, I am reminded that there is only one me in this world. Only one me who can be John's wife, the way I am. Only one me who can put words together in that certain way, or take that photograph, or make my grandmother's eyes light up that way. And only one me who can create this scrapbook page about the life that only I live. And that is a gift.

"Nurture"
by Heather Preckel

cardboard, ink (Ranger), floss (Making Memories), buttons (Junkitz), gaffer tape (7gypsies), transparency (Creative Imaginations), letters (Imagination Project), pen (EK Success), computer font (Times New Roman by Microsoft)

"To Learn"
by Cory Richardson-Lauve

paper (Making Memories), letters (Chatterbox, Basic Grey, My Mind's Eye, The Paper Loft), rub-ons (Scenic Route, Basic Grey), sticker (Cloud 9 Design), digital supplies (Two Peas in a Bucket, Scrapartist, Shabby Shoppe, Digital Scrapbook Memories)

work & play
family & friends
time apart
&
time together
spirituality & practicality

work out & relax
control & letting go
being a rock & having needs

living a beautiful
life & rejoicing
in the creativity of a mess

l i f e

balance

IN EVERY THING

"Balance"
by Katja Kromann

digital supplies (Katja Kromann), computer font (CheltPressDark 2.0)

thanks

giving

stillness

time alone

together

reading writing saving spending...

BALANCE

thinking feeling

family

CREATE

TIME

joy

activity

receiving

inspire

"Balance"
by Cory Richardson-Lauve

paper (Foof-a-La, My Mind's Eye), rub-ons (7gypsies, Basic Grey), stamp (Magnetic Poetry), ink (Color Box), stickers (K&Co, Scrapworks), computer font (Kravitz)

"It Happened Here"
by April Oaks

computer fonts (Goudy Old Style, Hotel Corral Essex), digital supplies including stitching (Digital Scrapbook Memories)

When did it happen? When did I decide for myself what I wanted in life? When did I learn for myself what I truly believed in? My parents, grandparents, leaders and teachers helped mold my testimony for a long time but eventually I had to learn for myself what was true. At 14 I specifically remember a powerful answer that helped me know for myself that what I had been taught was right. Still, even though I knew what was right and what I should be doing I had fun rebelling in High School. I was never very bad but I can't look back at the things I did wrong and feel any pride. Now I can see how easy it would have been for me to choose a different path in life. I am so glad I didn't.

Moving to the Tetons for the summer was a big turning point in my life. I had the freedom to do anything I wanted. No one was there to tell me no. I was able to decide on my own that I liked doing things that would lead me back to Heavenly Father. I liked doing things that were good. I wanted a happy life and I knew doing what was right would make me happy. I loved going to church in the Tetons. I felt the spirit there so strong. It was easy to reflect on what I had learned during the following week because everything was surrounded with reminded me of my ultimate goal to return to live with God. I was surrounded by parties and drugs in the dorm and it was easy to feel the contrast between that and the feelings I had at church. On my days off I would usually go hiking, swimming, boating, or camping. God's love seems to scream from every corner of the Tetons. When I think back on all the fun things I did in there I feel so happy. I will always have such happy memories there. My summers were full of fun. We laughed a lot. We were always having fun and I love remembering the exciting things we did. I'm grateful for the decision I made there to be the person I am today. I'm glad I did good things while I was there so I can look back on my experiences and smile.

Grand Teton National Park

It happened here in my favorite place

1993-1994

"This Changes Me"
by Cory Richardson-Lauve

paper (Polar Bear Press, My Mind's Eye, Foof-a-La), stickers (Polar Bear Press, Mrs. Grossman's, SEI, Chatterbox, Junkitz), stamps (Magnetic Poetry, Creative Imaginations), ink (Tim Holtz), acrylic paint (Folk Art), computer font (Broken 15)

you are my closest friend, who constantly challenges me to grow to strengthen to commit, to forgive, to laugh to love.

this changes ME.

you are the person I define myself with, and define myself against.

you are my partner on this journey. you change me.

This life is most amazing... I look at it every day and marvel that God has chosen to bless (us) so abundantly. Twenty years of love & happiness. There is no where I would rather be than right here where we are. You three are so very special to me. When we're together there is nothing that can compare. I love our life. I love our love. I love it all and I hope I never forget to be so very thankful for all the blessings of this life and all that we have.

what a Wonderful world

family

"Family" by Kelly Lautenbach

patterned papers (7gypsies), chipboard letters (Heidi Swapp for Advantus), chipboard swirls (Fancy Pants Designs), computer font (Chatterbox True Love)

Sometimes I feel like I see the world through a zoom lens - all up close and intimate. I notice all the details.

i see

gifts.

the tiniest things other people don't notice or value. But mostly, I see the gifts. All the

little images & connections that make this world

absolutely magical. There is so much to see. So much to know. So much to embrace.

"I See" by Cory Richardson-Lauve

digital supplies (Shabby Shoppe, Digital Scrapbook Memories, Katie Pertiet for Designer Digitals), computer fonts (CheltPress Trial, Adler)

"Lost and Found"
by Danielle Catalano-Titus

computer fonts (Weathered SF, Harting), digital supplies (Something Blue Studios)

"This Sacred Place"
by Cory Richardson-Lauve

computer fonts (LainieDaySH, Lithos Pro, L by Markus Schröppel), paper (My Mind's Eye), brads (Making Memories), rub-ons (Basic Grey), silk flowers (Michaels)

"Living Color/Shades of Grey" by Jessie Baldwin

acrylic paint (Folk Art Artist's Pigment [Plaid] in Aqua, Yellow Citron, Napthol Crimson, Cobalt Blue, Medium Yellow, Hauser Green Medium, Pure Orange, and Pure Black), embroidery thread (DMC), buttons (Scrap Arts), pens (Pilot G2 Gel Roller [Black], Uniball Signo [White])

**"Life"
by Cory Richardson-Lauve**

digital supplies (Shabby Shoppe, ScrapArtist, Katie Pertiet for Designer Digitals, Something Blue Studios), computer font (Lucida Sans)

"Precious"
by Barb Hogan

cardstock (Worldwin Papers), patterned papers (A2Z Essentials), coasterboard letters and rings (Gin-X by Imagination Project), brads (Making Memories), ink (Colorbox), pens (Uniball Signo, Sharpie by Sanford, Galaxy Markers by American Crafts), dimensional paint (Scribbles)

"Remember"
by Cory Richardson-Lauve

computer fonts (Lucida Sans, 1942 Report), digital supplies (Scrapartist)

If you would have shown me this photograph ten years ago, all I would have seen was two boys holding hands and walking down a dirt road. But at this point in my life, it all means so much more. I look at this picture and see my two sons four years apart in age and each with such different personalities truly enjoying each other's company. I see a big brother who is caring, sweet, thoughtful and always watching out for his little brother. I see a little brother who is funny, affectionate, charming and desperately trying to grow into a boy by following every move his older brother makes. I sometimes worry about their age difference and hope that they will not just get along, but truly enjoy being brothers. I pray that these two boys will grow to love each other unconditionally and always look out for each other's best interests. They will share a childhood filled with love, memories, fun, secrets and so much more which only the two of them can truly understand. This bond they will share will be special and different and truly one of a kind.

"Sharing a Childhood"
by Ursula Page

paper and stickers (Polar Bear Press), chipboard hearts (Heidi Swapp), rub-ons (7gypsies, Gin-X by Imagination Project, Junkitz, Autumn Leaves), brads (Making Memories, Joann's Scrap Essentials), ribbon

this is *Love*.

i believe real love: invites stays talks nurtures challenges gives plays celebrates hopes shares encourages discovers respects releases works creates waits survives

"This Is Love"
by Cory Richardson-Lauve

computer font (Aldine401 BT), digital supplies (Shabby Shoppe, Something Blue Studios, Scrapartist), rub-ons (Basic Grey, Autumn Leaves, Daisy D's), stickers (Foof-a-La, Me and My Big Ideas, Scrapworks, Kelly Panacci), ink (Colorbox)

A CELEBRATORY EXPERIENCE

Project: To create a scrapbook journal page that recognizes and celebrates your uniqueness.

> *Our inner world is a complex, exquisite, and powerful play of colors, lights, and shadows, a cathedral of consciousness as glorious as the natural world itself. This inner wealth is what the artist expresses.*
>
> —Julia Cameron

1. Start by making a list (mental or written) of things that you would not give up. They can be physical, emotional, or spiritual things. Then reflect on these questions:

   Why are they important to you?

   What is precious about them?

   How do they illustrate who you are?

2. Select some photographs, colors, and words that portray these things that are important to you. With some basic ideas in mind, draw a quick sketch of a page, if that helps you. Then begin your page. Use mediums (paint, paper, stitching, stamps, markers, stickers, digital technology) that express *you!* Add embellishments or supporting images as you work.

   Remember: Scrapbooking is a way to define yourself, and your creation is unique to you. Make choices only *you* would make. Avoid scraplifting (copying a layout someone else designed) because it dulls your creativity. It's okay to use other layouts for inspiration, but keep moving. The tiniest element—a photo corner, ribbon, or

7-1. "Nurture" by Heather Preckel (see color insert).

7-2. "Balance" by Katja Kromann (see color insert).

7-3. "It Happened Here" by April Oaks (see color insert).

7-4. "Family" by Kelly Lautenbach (see color insert).

color combination—might spark your imagination, but let your creative spirit lead you down your own path. Let your page evolve as you work.

One reason I have included other artists' work in the color insert of this book is so you can enjoy the uniqueness and diversity of each person's scrapbook style. Notice:

- *Heather's homespun touches of embroidery floss and buttons. (See layout 7-1.)*
- *Katja's edgier look with the black frame around her page. (See layout 7-2.)*
- *How April lets the photographs and journaling become the focal point. (See layout 7-3.)*
- *Kelly's attention to detail, such as the tiny text behind the journaling and the numbers along the bottom edge. (See layout 7-4).*
- *Danielle's expressive journaling and focus on creative artwork. (See layout 7-5.)*
- *Jessie's unpredictable colors and use of texture (buttons and thread). (See layout 7-6.)*
- *Ursula's soft, warm style. (See layout 7-7.)*

Notice especially what attracts you, what techniques and materials you are drawn to, what your favorite elements are. As you try new things, pay attention to what is comfortable and attractive to you. These are the elements that will help define your style and illustrate who you are. Keep experimenting, but always listen to your inner voice. Your style will inevitably evolve to reflect who you are as an artist.

3. As you work on this scrapbook journal page, remain aware of the focal point and balance and movement.

4. Include your thoughts in the form of journaling.

> *As you reflect on what is important to you, give thanks to your Creator for each gift.*

> *As you represent each important piece on the page, keep asking yourself, "How does this contribute to who I am?"*

5. Continue working until you feel your page reflects something essential about you. Then consider how you would answer these questions if God were asking you:

> *Who are you?*

> *What are you doing with the gifts I have given to you?*

> *What really matters to you?*

> *What can you celebrate?*

> *How will you find me?*

7-5. "Lost and Found" by Danielle Catalano-Titus (see color insert).

7-6. "Living Color/Shades of Grey" by Jessie Baldwin (see color insert).

7-7. "Sharing a Childhood" by Ursula Page (see color insert)

If you'd like to see how Barb Hogan and I interpreted this celebratory exercise, see "Precious" and "Remember" on the color insert. Barb's layout, "Precious," features energetic, effusive color. My layout, "Remember," makes prominent use of text and symbolic photos.

Going Deeper

Additional exercises in self-acceptance.

> *What lies behind us and what lies before us are tiny matters compared to what lies within us.*
>
> —RALPH WALDO EMERSON

✳ Sit down with some magazines. Page through them and tear out images that appeal to you at the moment: a swatch of color, a child's face, a sunset, or a beautiful kitchen. Then use the torn pages to make a collage on a scrapbook page.

✳ Create a scrapbook page about something you have done in your life that was 100 percent, completely you.

✳ Create a scrapbook page about a place in the world that you would like to visit alone.

✳ Create a page using some unique photographs you have taken. As you build your page, think about how your individual way of seeing the world contributes to your sense of self and sense of others.

✳ Make a scrapbook page about five items you would want if you were stranded on a desert island.

✳ Create a scrapbook page about four things you love about your body—two from below the neck, and two from above the neck!

Notes ———————

A Voice along the Journey

AMY M. BEATTY

This is what I love most about scrapbooking: I am part of a community of storytellers.

As a consultant for a direct marketing company, I enjoy the perks of products and profits. I enjoy the craft and the creativity. But for me, it's mostly about the people I have met and the stories I have heard and read.

No matter the style of scrapbooking, the purpose of an album is to tell a story. When I see layout samples in magazines or online galleries, I strain to read the tiny journaling and learn a little bit about the story of the person who created the page. As I create my own albums, I relive my stories. I feel the joy of the moment all over again as I create my layouts using pictures, words, papers, stickers, paint, or a variety of embellishments. The end result is that part of me and part of my life are now out there for me and others to see and enjoy.

Scrapbooking really took off for me when my friend Rachael and I began getting together once a month to scrapbook. We got lots of pages done, but, more important, we started a community and began to know each other better. (When Rachael brought her mother-in-law to scrapbook with us, it was as if I already knew her because I had read her story in Rachael's albums!)

When we give our albums to others, the sense of community expands. What better gift is there than the story of time spent together? We not only share ourselves, but we also include others in the community. One of my favorite projects was an album I made for my grandparents of our family trip to the beach. They enjoy reading it, and they enjoy sharing it with their friends. One day it will come back to me, and I will relive our special connection all over again.

8

Connection
Sharing Community

Art is about sharing: you wouldn't become an artist
unless you wanted to share an experience, a
thought.

—DAVID HOCKNEY

Who are the people that appear most often on your scrap-
book pages?
Who are the people with whom you share your pages?
How does scrapbooking draw you toward community?
How does scrapbooking connect you with God?

When you look at someone's scrapbook, it doesn't take long to
recognize who the important people are in that person's life.
Scrapbooking is a window into our deepest connections. Every
scrapbook page we create makes clear what is dearest to us
about people and relationships.

Scrapbooking propels us toward community. It allows us to
express our love and affection for others. It reminds us that we
have companions on this journey. It affirms our deepest connections with our loved ones and with God.

Nurturing Community

*If you were all alone in the universe with no one to
talk to, no one with which to share the beauty of
the stars, to laugh with, to touch, what would be
your purpose in life? It is other life, it is love, which
gives your life meaning. This is harmony.
We must discover the joy of each other, the joy of
challenge, the joy of growth.*

—MITSUGI SAOTOME

We are connected to each other in infinite and complicated ways.
Although we each walk alone, we experience the fullness of life
only with other human beings. Self-knowledge and self-definition
can only take us so far. Then we need to leap. We need to leap
into community.

The word *community* comes from the Latin word *communion*, meaning "mutual participation" or "sharing in common."
This is one of the gifts of life: we are here together. But our culture teaches a myth of separation that is fed by competition and
invisible borders. Our constant task is to recognize our need for
others and nurture our connections.

When I think back over my life about the times when I've felt
most "connected," a memory of working at a summer camp
comes immediately to mind.

We had walked down the forested trail to the fire circle at
dusk, encouraging our campers to leave their flashlights off and
trust the people walking ahead of them. We heard an occasional
snicker or whisper, but mostly it was silent except for the crunch-
ing of leaves underfoot. As we gathered, we formed a circle and
began singing. We then settled quietly onto benches around the
logs waiting to be lit.

The nighttime sounds of the forest were all that we heard as
the camp director, Bob, prepared to light the fire. Tiny flames
grasped for tinder and the light grew, illuminating the circle of

faces that had become so familiar over the past weeks and months. Campers and counselors took turns telling stories about the past two weeks: hiking miles along the Appalachian Trail, canoeing on the James River, stargazing in the field, singing in the dining hall after meals, and playing games in the field at sunset.

As the fire reached its fullness and began to settle into glowing coals, we, the counselors, used tubs of warm water to wash the feet of our campers and each other. These were feet that needed washing—feet that had spent weeks in sports shoes and hiking boots, feet that were healing from blisters and sunburns. Some resisted at first, but most realized the metaphor. We were serving each other. We were there for each other in the darkness, facing the dirtiest, most undesirable parts of each other. Tomorrow we would say goodbye. But we would not forget the lessons we had learned and the importance of our connection.

Even though those nostalgic days of summer camp may be long gone, we each need to keep finding the "campfire communities" in our lives. What songs do we sing to give us courage and strength? What stories do we tell each other? Whose feet do we wash? Whom do we let wash our feet? And, most important, how do we maintain the strength of the fire so we can feel warmth, scare away the darkness, and truly see each other?

I nurture several campfire communities in my life—my family and friends, of course, and the close-knit community in which we live and work—but one of the strongest of these is a group of scrapbookers, many of whom I have yet to meet in person.

In the spring of 2005, after winning honorable mentions in a prominent scrapbooking contest, several of us gathered online to establish a private message board. After several months of "talking," we all decided that *not* winning the contest was the best thing that could have happened to us. The judges' decision had brought us together: a diverse and dynamic group of people who had come together as scrapbookers and stayed together as friends. We share stories about our struggles with relationships, our parenting challenges and celebrations, our scrapbooking accomplishments and disappointments, and our artistic experiments and successes. We post pages to share with one another and

My card. You can see in the background the completed card file, with the cards from the other members of the community.

grow closer as we learn about each woman's family and faith and values. We praise each other's artwork and give constructive criticism when it is requested. We offer career and industry advice and solace during the frustrating times. We cry and laugh together.

I have one tangible, physical symbol of our little online community: a card file. Each of us created a tiny symbol of ourselves by making a scrapbook-style card decorated with artwork, images, and words that reflect our personality. We re-created the card for each member of the group and shared them with each other. The cards reflect our diversity: a variety of colors and styles, digital and paper techniques; some with ribbons, some sleek, and some silly. All perfect.

You never know where you will find a campfire community. But I do know that scrapbooking, which has led me to more surprises than I can name, has introduced me to a rich community that shares *"the joy of each other, the joy of challenge, the joy of growth."*

Expanding Connections

Somewhere, there are people to whom we can speak with passion without having the words catch in our throats. Somewhere a circle of hands will open to receive us, eyes will light up as we enter, voices will celebrate with us whenever we come into our own power.

—STARHAWK

In 2006 a friend of mine opened her digital scrapbooking website, and it all came into focus for me—what this endeavor of scrapbooking is all about, the connections and the sharing. Kristie is one of the most generous people I've met online, and her website for The Shabby Shoppe is an extension of herself (see Appendix B). She creates a warm, soft, aesthetically beautiful environment for digital scrapbookers who want to gather and share their work and ideas. It is easy

to get bogged down in the "industry" of scrapbooking (the publishing, marketing, and newest products), but that is eclipsed by the elements of communion: finding energy and inspiration as we connect with other scrapbookers through our images and words.

I feel such warmth when I read books by other scrapbookers. They invite me into their lives with their artwork and conversational writing. I feel my world expand as I examine Rebecca Sower's lovingly stitched pages, see the way Stacy Julian meaningfully organizes her layouts and albums, or read Cathy Zielske's candid journaling. Their creations feed me in ways I didn't even know I hungered for. (See Appendix B for more information about these books.)

Several years ago, after feeling grateful for this feeling of community, I created the layout above. Notice that it celebrates not only scrapbooking connections, but music and books that have changed me as well. The journaling reads:

> *Well, none of you know me. I don't really know*
> *you either, just the parts of you that you've*
> *chosen to share with the world. But each of you*
> *has changed or significantly enriched my life in*

some profound way. Because of you, I am more
spiritual. I am more expressive. I am more grate-
ful. Because of you I am more alive. Thank you
for your music, your insight, your creativity,
your openness, your hopefulness. It is a blessing
to be on this earth with you. I hope we will meet
someday.

Knowing that we have companions on this journey is a crucial element of community. I think one of the reasons I was drawn to submitting my pages for publication is because I wanted somehow to join the community of scrapbookers that I was getting to know through their layouts in magazines. They inspired me with their creativity and vision, taught me new techniques, and challenged me to be more artistic and more myself. I wanted to know these women.

Of course, having a few pages published did not connect me in some magical way with the hundreds of other scrapbookers who had the same fortune to catch some magazine editor's eye. But it did help me figure out what kind of artist I wanted to be and it gave me the confidence to define my work and voice, which led to new connections and opportunities that I could not have imagined.

When I am scrapbooking, I know that I am not alone. I know that others will recognize what is beautiful in me, that others are struggling, too—in things as little as creative block and as large as accepting the loss of people they love.

If you're looking for ways to move into the scrapbooking community, consider some of these options:

- Take a class.
- Enter a contest.
- Connect with others through message boards or your local scrapbook store.
- Crop with your neighbors, friends, or family.
- Share your pages with friends, post them in online galleries, and offer them for publication.

- Make time to see other scrapbookers' pages in online galleries, in magazines, or locally.
- Teach a class.
- Create gift books or layouts for others.
- Use your gift—writing, photography, or design—to inspire others.

When we move beyond creating pages cloistered in our homes to sharing in the larger community that includes other scrapbookers throughout the world, we tap into the energy of companions who are fed by the same pursuit. As we bring our ideas to a common table, we nourish and care for each other. We are not just working alongside each other, but we are also inspiring and serving each other. What brings us together can be a million different things—but what holds us together is our shared experience. The community of scrapbookers nurtures the creativity in all of us.

Expressing Affection

There is nothing more truly artistic
than to love people.

—VINCENT VAN GOGH

When I watch the teenagers I work with, I am amazed by how easy it is for them to touch one another. One of my regrets about not having small children in my life over the past few years is the absence of their easy affection. Young children throw themselves at you for hugs and snuggles, and don't hesitate to climb up onto your lap or clasp your leg. Teenagers, after they've been together for a few days, are like this with each other. Affection and horseplay are frequent and natural. But, as their caregiving adult, I need to be more cautious. I need to maintain a balance between warmth and professionalism.

Scrapbooking allows me to break down some of those boundaries.

John and I have always loved being outside. We love the adventures, the sights and smells, and the rawness of being surrounded by creation. On this November day we drove to the Blue Ridge Parkway with the 4 girls living in our home. We never left the sight of the parkway, but it was an adventure for them. And at the end of the day...a beautiful sunset. 2003

sharing nature.

A layout about a trip we took to the Blue Ridge Parkway ... we saw the sunset and the moonrise. John and I shared our love for nature with our girls, many of whom had never walked a trail or driven along a mountain road.

We have two girls leaving next week. Ella and Tonya are going to live with their families, which is our ultimate goal. So I am happy—but sad, too. We've spent more than a year sharing the journey with each of these girls, and I will miss them. I will miss Ella's intelligence and quick smile. I will miss Tonya's ability to make me laugh and her willingness to learn. I will miss their faces and habits. I will miss their presence.

Because hellos and goodbyes are an integral part of the work that John and I do, I create rituals that help me stop and notice. I always wait until the last week before a girl departs to complete a farewell scrapbook album. In this case, I know it will be a late-night marathon of completing their albums, but I need to do this. I go through photographs on my computer and choose the special ones. I remember the good times: posing along the Blue Ridge Parkway ... at the National Zoo ... playing with hairstyles ... sharing laughter and hugs. It is so good to remember the moments that eclipse the struggles. I take my time with these memories, remembering, crying, and giving thanks. It is closure for me.

In moments like this one, scrapbooking allows us to step back and see the larger picture, to savor the brush we've had with another soul, to bask in our connection. In creating albums to give away, we are also expressing our gratitude to another for sharing his or her life. But it is more than that. We get to keep so much! We are fed by our memories of the best parts of the people we love, by their smiles and their spirits. These scrapbooks are not just something we give to others; in the process of creating them, we receive the gift of growing closer to those we love.

Ultimately, it is our connections that matter most. I can say, "I am an artist, a seamstress, a writer, a gardener, a photographer, a scrapbooker." But all of that self-definition is only the beginning. I firmly believe that the only thing that can truly change us is our relationships with each other. We grow by being faithful, by recovering from deceit, by being inspired, by suffering loss, by loving. And we need to be in community with others to grow in these ways. Each time we create a scrapbook page, we are making connections. The process itself leads us to consider how people, events, and time are linked. In the end, what truly matters is that we are all connected—to each other, and to the great source of life and light and hope we call God.

Connecting with Spirit

Prayer is when you talk to God;
meditation is when you listen to God.

—Diana Robinson

Scrapbooking is both talking and listening; it can be both prayer and meditation.

I have often thought that scrapbooking is a holy experience because of the way it celebrates life and expresses our truest and most intimate feelings. Scrapbooking can be a prayer of gratitude because it helps us notice the little things in life. We become aware of colors and shadows; we see the nuances of skin tones and seasons. Scrapbooking reminds us to embrace all the gifts of life. When we can listen and wait in faith, not taking for granted the beauty and love that surround us, every page can be a prayer of gratefulness that connects us with our Source.

Scrapbooking helps us embrace every moment, not just the fantastically exciting or stimulating ones, but also the sad and the moving times. In times of concern or grieving, scrapbooking can be a prayer of supplication, as we hold our loved ones close. Scrapbooking brings the people we care for, or have lost, to the foreground in both literal and figural ways. As we focus on our connection, we are, in a very real sense, praying for the people who are important to us, honoring them and celebrating them.

Scrapbooking can also be a meditative experience that quiets the mind as we release our fears and worries and to-do lists. When my body and mind become absorbed with a visual focus, with balance, with color, with expression, scrapbooking becomes a form of meditation for me. Nothing else matters except for the placement of paper and image, and I lose myself in the material and open myself to the process.

As Robert Benson writes:

> *We cannot be filled with God until we are not so full of ourselves.... We cannot give our hearts to God, or anyone else for that matter, as long as they are too heavy for us to lift.*
>
> *... It is an ongoing process of being willing to present ourselves to God as we are, over and over again. This step in the Dance, faithfully and honestly and regularly observed, is what creates the space for the Word to be clearly and joyfully heard within us, and then without us as well.*[1]

When I am alone in my scrapbook space, I like to set a timer so I can avoid looking at the clock. Then I can work until the next chore or meeting beckons. I am always surprised when the timer goes off because I have usually forgotten that anything else exists but the paper and words in front of me. The paper and photographs in my hands have eased me into a rhythm, and I have moved outside of myself and beyond my worries. I am free—free in God's time, in God's boundless space.

In its highest form, scrapbooking is holy: an expression of our truest and most intimate selves, an honoring of moments, a celebration of the journey of life and living. When we share our pages with others, scrapbooking connects us with God through each other. We see through each other's eyes and behold each other's gifts.

How will you celebrate the connections in your life? What will you create on your next page?

A CONNECTING EXPERIENCE

Project: To create a scrapbook journal page that honors a relationship that touches you deeply.

There is no hope of joy except in human relations.

—Antoine de Saint-Exupery

1. Start by considering the communities in your life:

Your household

Your extended family

Your dearest friends

Your place of worship, neighborhood, or town

Your state, nation, or world

2. Choose a relationship from one of these communities that touches you. It can be a connection with someone you know well or with someone you observe from afar. It can be an intriguing connection between other people that you'd like to explore more fully. The important thing is to select a connection that contains something you value. Then find some photographs or images that represent this connection.

8-1

3. Design a page that reflects the nature of this connection. Here are some techniques you can use to make "connection" visible:

8-2

8-3

8-4

- *Choose pictures from different events or eras that are connected in some way. (See layout 8-1.)*
- *Layer words on top of your image. (See layout 8-2.)*
- *Repeat patterns or motifs. (See layout 8-3.)*
- *Repeat sizes. (See layout 8-4.)*
- *Overlap photographs. (See layout 8-5.)*
- *Write about what the pictures mean to you. (See layout 8-6.)*

4. Once you have some basic ideas in mind for your page, draw a quick sketch, if that helps you. Remember: It is not necessary to plan all the details of your page, just to start with an intentional idea. You can add other embellishments or supporting images as you work.

5. Begin your page. Use whatever mediums please you (paint, paper, stitching, stamps, markers, stickers, digital technology). Be open to creative ideas as they come. Even though you started with a rough plan, your page will evolve as you work.

6. Remain aware of the focal point and balance and movement.

7. Include your thoughts in the form of journaling.

Use these questions to help you explore the connection you are honoring:

What are the elements of this relationship?

How does this relationship teach you about connection?

What do you value about this particular connection?

8-5

8. Continue working until you feel your page communicates the essence of your connection. Then give yourself some time to reflect on these questions:

What can you learn from this connection?

What elements of this connection can you bring into other relationships in order to strengthen them?

How does this connection bring you closer to God?

8-6

If you'd like to see how Ursula Page and I interpreted this connecting exercise, see "Sharing a Childhood" and "This Is Love" on the color insert.

Going Deeper

Additional exercises in connecting.

When we seek for connection, we restore the world to wholeness. Our seemingly separate lives become meaningful as we discover how truly necessary we are to each other.

—MARGARET WHEATLEY

✳ How do you experience community in your life? Make a scrapbook page about your different communities, such as family, work, friends, and place of worship.

✳ How has your community of family changed over the course of your life? Think about your childhood family and your present family (nuclear family, group of friends, or marriage). How are they alike? How are they different? What are the values of each community? Use photos to illustrate your comparisons.

✳ Create a page documenting your family tree.

✳ Choose three random photos. Create a scrapbook page exploring how they are connected.

✳ Start a scrapbook for the family/community in which you live. Keep it in a prominent area with an instant camera nearby. Encourage your family members/roommates/guests to add spontaneous pictures and words.

✳ Pick one small random item (such as a leaf, a steering wheel, a baby's pacifier, an electrical outlet) and take a picture of it. Then journal about it: Why is it important in this world? What is its contribution? What connections does it symbolize?

✳ Create a scrapbook page that reflects your connection with God.

Techniques and Supplies

CARDSTOCK

Cardstock is the most basic scrapbook supply. In its simplest use, it provides a resting place for the eyes. Here are some other ways to work with cardstock:

- Choose a cardstock that is the same color as your photo's focal point to draw out color from your photo.
- Use a cardstock color that contrasts with your photograph(s) for a livelier page.
- Use cardstock for framing photographs, journaling blocks, or the page itself.
- Make shapes out of cardstock, such as circles, waves, or repeated squares, lines, or rectangles, to create movement.
- Use pieces of cardstock for journaling blocks. (This is handy if you make a mistake; you can just cut a new piece.)

ACCENTS

Anything on a page outside of the photographs, the cardstock, and the title is considered an accent. In the latest issue of one of my favorite scrapbooking magazines, I found all of these items used as accents: patterned paper, stamped images, die cuts, ribbon, stitching, stickers, flowers, jewels and gems, digital brushes, metals, bookplates, labels, initials, brads, buttons, paper clips, doodles, tags, embossing powders, safety pins, charms, painted images, rub-ons, rhinestones, felt shapes, rickrack, staples, glitter, microbeads, and chipboard shapes and letters.

Accents can be fickle; they come and go with the trends. Introducing new accents is one of the ways we show that we are journeying through life, not just standing still in a particular year. But no matter which accents we use, we need to use them purposefully. Think of a flower in your garden. It is beautiful and decorative, but so much more. With its fragrance and color, it attracts moths and bees, so that pollination can take place and continue the life cycle of the flower. The vibrant petals point inward, toward the heart of the flower, where the pollen awaits. Insects are directed there by subtle and not-so-subtle hints. Likewise, accents look pretty, but they can and should serve a purpose on our pages. They can add meaning, movement, emphasis, balance, and interest. Keep these ideas in mind:

- Use accents to draw attention to the focal point photo or title—to create a line toward the focal point or to encircle or point to the focal point.

- Use accents to anchor a photo, to create a frame, or to add photo corners.

- Use accents to balance a strong picture or journaling block.

- Use accents to create movement. Remember the visual triangle: three accents or groups of accents arranged in a triangle will draw the viewer's eye across the page. Lines of images or strips of paper will also draw the eye.

- Use accents to emphasize your message. Use quotation stickers, stamped words, or themed accents to underscore the meaning behind your page.

- Use accents to give more information about the page, such as date, place, or names.

- Use accents to add texture so your page will appeal to the sense of touch as well as sight. Add elements that are smooth, soft, fine, rough, silky, bumpy, or coarse.

- Use accents to add interest to a layout. Avoid overpowering your focal point, but give your viewer something else to look at as well. A small cluster of two or three accents can add interest to a layout that has a single photo and cardstock.

- Use accents to add variety to a layout. If you love black-and-white photos, introduce other colors through your accents. If you love square and rectangular photographs, use circle shapes as accents. If you tend to crop your photographs to the same size, use a variety of sizes in your accents.

- Use accents to serve a physical function. Attach, hang, conceal, and lift with accents.

STAMPS AND INKS

Stamps and inks can add wonderful dimension to your pages. I've struggled with buying stamps because they are expensive and cumbersome to store. But with the advent of clear acrylic stamps over the past couple of years, at least one of these problems is solved. Clear acrylic stamps are thin and light, and they can be stored flat in binders or CD cases. They adhere temporarily to acrylic blocks when you use them and then can be peeled off for storage. Because you can see through them, clear stamps make it easy to position your design on the page. With rubber and wooden mounted stamps, you have to guess. Although part of the charm of stamping is its imperfection, I still want my letters to be aligned. So I love clear stamps! And you can buy them in a variety of sizes, patterns, and alphabet fonts.

Choose a variety of stamps in designs that appeal to you. It is good to have an assortment of fonts, but the cost of letter stamps can really add up. To stay within your budget, buy the simplest fonts first and be wary of ultra-trendy styles. They will likely go out of fashion quickly. Downloading trendy fonts is an alternative to buying the more pricey stamps.

Choose ink colors that appeal to you and coordinate with the paper colors you use often. Mini ink pads are an inexpensive way to experiment with color. You can also investigate inks for different surfaces; some inks are best suited for paper, while others are better if you want to stamp on metal or other non-porous surfaces. Ask for guidance at your local craft, scrapbooking, or stamping store.

Here are some ways to use stamps on your pages:

- Stamp a title or part of a title.
- Stamp the journaling (if you are really diligent, or if your journaling is short).
- Add shape by stamping a pattern on your background paper.
- Stamp a border to draw attention to your focal point or to create unity. (Stamp around the outside edges of a two-page layout.)
- Stamp a word in different levels of saturation to add repetition and variety.
- Stamp a cluster of images to create an embellishment.
- Stamp on an embellishment such as a paper flower or a metal photo corner.
- Stamp on top of a photo to fill an empty space.
- Stamp a repeated pattern to create movement.
- Stamp the date on a layout.
- Create your own patterned paper strips.
- Stamp on a transparency, and layer over other embellishments such as rub-ons or stickers.
- Stamp on large letters or monograms.
- Rub brown ink on an embellishment that needs to be muted.
- Rub ink along the edges of your layout or along individual elements to create contrast and unity.
- Apply ink directly to the paper (instead of to a stamp) to create a colorful background.
- Use a stencil and ink to create shapes on your page.
- Use stamps and/or ink to add a color that will help balance your page.

- Stamp an image and then draw, doodle, or stitch around it.
- Stamp into embossing powder or clay for dimension.
- Use stamps to reinforce your theme.

One of the best tips I've learned for inking stamps is to turn the stamp over (hold it in your hand with the image facing up) and use the ink in your other hand (facing down) to blot the stamp with ink. That lets you see how much ink you are applying and keeps you from getting ink on the edges of your stamp, where it might transfer extra marks onto your paper (again, part of the charm—but frustrating if you are on the last letter of a long, very neat word).

My favorite stamps are those with script or text blocks; they add interest and sometimes meaning, and can be used on a variety of layouts. Geometric shapes are also a good investment, making it easy to create a line of shapes for repetition.

ADDING WORDS

When you plan the writing on your pages, think about your purpose. Are you writing so others can read it? If so, then use an easily legible serif or sans-serif font and adjust the leading (the space between lines) to make it more readable. Save the scripts and decorative fonts for titles and artistic touches. If you want writing to be part of the *artwork* of the page, and your purpose is more in the act of writing than in having it be readable, then play around with fonts and handwriting. Let the function dictate your form.

There are hundreds, if not thousands, of free fonts that can be downloaded from the Internet. (Search "free fonts.") Resist the urge to collect them all; instead, choose the ones that appeal most to you. One way to limit your supply is to download only one font for every page or project you complete. Then you will slowly amass a meaningful font library and prevent font overload. It can be difficult to wade through excess.

I store an extra folder of fonts in "My Documents" on my hard drive, separate from where they are installed in Windows.

This way I can easily back them up and reinstall them in the event of a crash or if I need to reformat my computer.

SEWING

Sewing can add wonderful texture and interest to a layout. You can use a sewing machine or stitch by hand to:

- Add emphasis by framing your focal point.
- Add movement by creating horizontal or vertical lines, waves, or shapes.
- Add balance by using colorful thread.
- Emphasize an important part of a photograph.
- Draw lines under text.
- Attach items to your layout.
- Create embellishments, such as flowers or swirls.
- Create a "finished" look on a page by stitching around the edges of cardstock or patterned paper.
- Unify several elements by stitching around them (creating a border).
- Create a sense of unity by repeating the stitching motif several times on the page.
- Create a "quilted" background or an accent.
- Add contrast with thread color.

If you are stitching by hand, experiment with different threads, flosses, and ribbons. Pierce your paper with a pushpin before stitching to make it easier to sew. (Start with a ruler line drawn in pencil if you want straight or evenly spaced stitches. Erase the line after piercing the holes and before stitching.)

If you are stitching with a machine, experiment with different stitches and stitch lengths. Test your machine's setting on scrap paper of a similar thickness before stitching the actual page. Adjust tension and stitch length, if necessary. If you are nervous about stitching directly on your page, stitch on a photograph or a separate piece of paper and then adhere it to your page. It will look as though you stitched it to the page.

PAINT

I tend to dislike anything messy, so it is rare that I pull out the paint on a layout. But there are rewards that make the mess worthwhile. Paint is a great way to add texture and color. But, more than that, it allows you to experience the creative process at a sensory level. You will get paint on your fingers. And paint will move and swirl to become what you want it to be. Explore different kinds of paint: acrylic, watercolors, fingerpaint. Here are some ways to use paint on your pages:

- Create backgrounds.
- Create repetition by painting blocks or lines.
- Edge the border of a layout or photograph with paint.
- Sew on top of a painted area.
- Paint over stickers or die cuts, then remove them. It will make an interesting silhouette.
- Use paint with stencils.
- Use paint to change the color of an embellishment or a piece of paper.

DIGITAL BRUSHES

Digital brushes are a tool in most photo-editing programs, such as Adobe Photoshop Elements. You can use them like a real paintbrush to draw, doodle, shade, or otherwise apply color to a page. More frequently, though, in digital scrapbooking, brushes are used like a stamp. Instead of dragging the cursor across the page, click once to make an impression on your page.

Brushes are an easy and versatile way to add interest to a photograph or to an entire layout. Here are some ways to use brushes:

- Draw attention to the focal point with swirls or frames.
- Add color.
- Print on a transparency and add it to a layout.
- Create patterned paper for backgrounds or accents.

- Repeat an element or a word in varying sizes and colors.

- Add emphasis or balance by using contrasting colors or shapes.

- Create movement with swirls, circles, dotted lines, or waves.

- Add texture by adjusting the opacity of brush layers.

- Use shapes to enhance the theme of your layout.

And here are some tips to keep in mind when you are creating brushes:

- Photoshop will not allow you to create a brush larger than 8 x 8 inches at 300 dpi. Reduce the size of your image, if necessary.

- Store your brushes in a folder in "My Documents." If you store all your brushes within a program such as Photoshop, performance slows down. When you want to use your brushes in Photoshop, choose "load brushes" and click on the brush you would like to use.

See Appendix B for recommended websites that provide tutorials on how to create and use brushes.

OTHER DIGITAL TECHNIQUES

When you enter the world of digital scrapbooking, you will learn something new every time you complete a page. You can use the digital medium to:

- Change the colors of elements.

- Change the opacity of elements to create a translucent or vellum-like look.

- Adjust the modes of the different layers to create depth, color, and luminosity.

- Easily change the size of different elements.

- Create flourishes, swirls, and other shapes.

- Easily edit text to change its content, size, font, or color.
- Adjust the brightness and clarity of photographs.
- Create frames around photographs.
- Duplicate photographs and embellishments.
- Apply filters that change the appearance of photographs.
- Print titles or other words on top of photographs.

See Appendix B for recommended digital tutorials.

Resources

MAGAZINES

Creating Keepsakes
Published monthly. www.creatingkeepsakes.com

Digital Scrapbooking
Published six times a year by *Simple Scrapbooks*.
www.digitalscrapbooking.com

Legacy
Published bimonthly. www.stampington.com/html/legacy.html

Memory Makers
Published nine times a year. www.memorymakersmagazine.com

Scrapbooks Etc.
Published eight times a year. www.bhgscrapbooksetc.com

Simple Scrapbooks
Published six times a year. www.simplescrapbooksmag.com

BOOKS ON SCRAPBOOKING

Edwards, Ali. *A Designer's Eye for Scrapbooking.* Escondido, CA: Primedia, 2004.

———. *A Designer's Eye for Scrapbooking with Patterned Paper.* Escondido, CA: Primedia, 2006.
Ali's books reflect her graphic design background and focus on telling stories. Her motto "Capture life. Create art," permeates her pages and her advice for scrapbookers. I love to look at her artful designs and be inspired to tell my own stories.

Julian, Stacy. *The Big Picture: Scrapbook Your Life and a Whole Lot More.* Bluffdale, UT: Simple Scrapbooks, 2005.
Stacy's book is a celebration of life with great practical instructions for scrapbooking. I immediately feel more passionate about scrapbooking—and life—every time I read it.

Sower, Rebecca. *Scrapbooking Life's Little Moments.* Escondido, CA: Primedia, 2004.

————. *Scrapbooking Life's Little Treasures.* Escondido, CA: Primedia, 2002.
Rebecca has a homespun yet elegant style that radiates gratefulness and faith. Her books drive me toward creativity and encourage me to write love letters to my friends and family on my layouts.

Zielske, Cathy. *Clean & Simple Scrapbooking: Ideas for Design, Photography, Journaling & Typography.* Escondido, CA: Primedia, 2004.

————. *Clean & Simple Scrapbooking: The Sequel: More Cool Ideas for the Simpler Side of Scrapbooking.* Bluffdale, UT: Simple Scrapbooks, 2006.
Cathy is a clean-lined scrapbooker and graphic designer. Her books are funny and instructive. I find myself becoming more expressive as a writer just from reading her frank and heartfelt journaling.

OTHER PLACES TO GO FOR INSPIRATION AND INSTRUCTION

www.bigpicturescrapbooking.com
This website builds on the philosophy of Stacy Julian's book and offers online classes taught by a variety of instructors. A great way to connect with the international scrapbooking community and learn new techniques.

Cameron, Julia. *The Artist's Way: A Spiritual Path to Creativity.* New York: J. P. Tarcher, 2002.
A best-selling book of insight and exercises to help you uncover your artistic self. I have completed the process a few different times in my life and have experienced remarkable creative growth and self-discovery each time.

www.fortheloveofeffers.blogspot.com
This site offers a weekly scrapbooking challenge that will push your creativity to new levels. I love visiting the blog to be inspired by the artwork of the four scrapbookers and guest artists who create and interpret "the dares."

www.shimelle.com
Shimelle offers inspiration on her blog, and she also teaches classes for a small fee. I participated in her Christmas art journal

class and loved the daily prompts and guidance that helped me make visible my Advent journey.

PHOTOGRAPHY

Patterson, Freeman. *Photography and the Art of Seeing: A Visual Perception Workshop for Film and Digital Photography.* Toronto: Key Porter Books, 2004.
This book is not about the mechanics of the camera, but the joy of immersing yourself in the process of photography. Covers design principles, color, and different ways of seeing and imagining.

Peterson, Bryan. *Understanding Exposure: How to Shoot Great Photographs with a Film or Digital Camera.* New York: Amphoto Books, 2004.
This book will help you understand the basic components of photography, including aperture, shutter speed, and ISO. I began using the manual settings on my camera soon after reading it.

DIGITAL SCRAPBOOKING AND PHOTOSHOP ELEMENTS TUTORIALS

www.theshabbyshoppe.com/tutorials/software_tutorials.asp
The Shabby Shoppe offers digital scrapbooking products (including several free downloads at www.shabbyprincess.com), a message board, a public gallery, and tutorials.

www.digitalscrapbookmemories.com/digitalscrapbooktips.asp
Digital Scrapbook Memories offers digital products on CD. This link will take you to tutorials that will help you with the basics of digital scrapbooking, such as understanding layers and printing layouts, as well as more advanced techniques, such as rounding corners and changing paper colors.

www.twopeasinabucket.com/digital.asp
The digital team at Two Peas in a Bucket offers digital products, tutorials, challenges, and answers to frequently asked questions.

www.graphicssoft.about.com/od/pselements
A non-scrapbooking site that teaches the basics of Adobe Photoshop Elements.

WRITING

Hale, Constance. *Sin and Syntax: How to Craft Wickedly Effective Prose*. New York: Broadway Books, 1999.
A review of basic grammar and composition written in an engaging, illustrative manner. I wrote some of my best scrapbooking journaling while reading this book.

Lamott, Anne. *Bird by Bird: Some Instructions on Writing and Life*. New York: Anchor, 1995.
A funny, frank, and extremely encouraging book on the writing process. This book was so enjoyable to read that I immediately went to the library to find the rest of Anne Lamott's books.

Ueland, Brenda. *If You Want to Write*. St. Paul: Gray Wolf Press, 1987.
A book that links writing with imagination and spirit. Its pleasantly meandering style reminds me of the joy in the process of writing and living.

Zinsser, William. *On Writing Well: The Classic Guide to Writing Nonfiction*. New York: HarperCollins, 2001.
A clear and concisely written book that provides instruction and advice to the nonfiction writer. I enjoy rereading it just for the author's mastery of language.

Contributors

JESSIE BALDWIN taught elementary school for several years and recently worked part-time as the art director for a local private school. She has now retired from teaching to focus on making art; raising her kids, Violet and Riley; and spending time with her husband, Rick. She considers each 12 x 12-inch page her "canvas" and proudly displays much of her art on the walls of her house, not in albums. Her work has been published in a variety of scrapbooking publications.

AMY M. BEATTY lives with her husband and son in Tennessee. She is a consultant for a scrapbooking company and loves getting to know her customers and their stories. She also teaches high school math.

DANIELLE CATALANO-TITUS spends her time outside of scrapbooking doing three things: being with her family (husband and two-year old daughter, Zoe, along with their two cats); being a high school art teacher; and directing a high school theater group. She teaches part-time, which allows her to scrapbook and operate her online digital scrapbooking store, Something Blue Studios.

BARB HOGAN spends her time juggling her family (husband, Andy; daughter, Shannon; and trusty canine, Olive), her creative job for a scrapbook manufacturer, a small photography business, and her other major pastime as a tae kwon do black-belt and instructor. She enjoys creating layouts with both digital and paper elements, and she says that while scrapbooking has brought many blessings into her life, she is most grateful for the friendships she's made all over the world.

KATJA KROMANN lives with her husband and son in California. She has been crafting all her life and enjoys creating everything from willow baskets to scrapbook pages. She is a published scrapbooking artist, member of several manufacturer design teams, and owner of Katja Kromann Design and Photography.

KELLY LAUTENBACH was named to the Creating Keepsakes Hall of Fame in 2006 after winning Honorable Mentions in 2004 and 2005. Her work is published in a variety of scrapbooking magazines. When she's not playing with paper and paste, she enjoys dabbling in the world of digital scrapbooking and thoroughly enjoys the challenge of combining the two art forms. She lives in Nebraska with the loves her life: her husband and teenage son and daughter.

APRIL OAKS lives in Utah. She is a digital scrapbooker who teaches classes around the country and owns Digital Scrapbook Memories. She has been featured on several news programs, in newspapers and magazines, and even on the radio as a promoter of digital scrapbooking. She is a mother of two, which she considers her greatest profession.

URSULA PAGE lives in Georgia with her family (husband Chris and children Sterling, Preston, and Harper). She loves watching the scrapbooking industry evolve and uses her spare moments to do freelance work for magazines. She has designed scrapbooking products, and her work has been published in various scrapbooking publications.

CATHY PASCUAL, a former communications professional, lives in the Seattle area and is a wife (to Jamie) and mother (to Sofia, age two). Cathy started scrapbooking after watching a QVC program on the topic and hasn't looked back since! Her layouts have been published in scrapbooking magazines and newsletters. In addition to scrapbooking, Cathy enjoys blogging, reading, baking with her daughter, and watching movies with her husband.

HEATHER PRECKEL resides in western North Carolina with her husband, daughter, and two dogs. She has been a passionate scrapbooker for more than seven years, and has been a member of more than a dozen design teams. She is also a published scrapbook artist and part-owner of A2Z.

KAREN RUSSELL grew up in southern Oregon and now lives in Grants Pass with her family, where she works part-time as a dental hygienist. She has always had a love of photography and began incorporating it into scrapbooking five years ago. She has traveled internationally as a scrapbooking instructor and designed products for manufacturers. Her work has been published in a variety of scrapbooking publications.

JESSICA SPRAGUE is a contributing editor to *Creating Keepsakes* magazine. She has a bachelor's degree in English, and is passionate about telling the stories of her life and leaving a legacy for her children of writing, photography, and design. She sees her pages (both digital and paper) as a way to let her children know what she believes in, to know that they are loved and valued, and to know that they have a meaningful heritage.

SHARYN TORMANEN has been married for fourteen years and has four children. She enjoys sewing, reading, rubber-stamping, and scrapbooking. She has always enjoyed the process of combining stories with pictures. In the past six years she's become more active in the publication side of scrapbooking and has shared her work with scrapbookers through numerous magazines and design team positions. But what she enjoys most about scrapbooking is the network available for sharing, and the friends she's made. And, of course, the reminder to treasure those everyday moments.

Notes

INTRODUCTION

1. Rainer Maria Rilke, *Letters to a Young Poet & The Possibility of Being* (New York: MJF Books, 2000), 35.

CHAPTER 1: RESONANCE

1. Madeleine L'Engle, *Glimpses of Grace: Daily Thoughts and Reflections* (New York: HarperCollins Publishers, 1996), 258.

CHAPTER 2: EQUILIBRIUM

1. National Space Biomedical Research Institute, "Inner Ear and Balance Issues," http://www.nsbri.org/EarthBenefits/Ear_Balance.html.
2. Kim Williams, "Symmetry in Architecture," http://members.tripod.com/vismath/kim.

CHAPTER 4: AWARENESS

1. Freeman Patterson, *Photography and the Art of Seeing* (Toronto: Key Porter Books, 2004).
2. Thomas Moore, *Dark Nights of the Soul: A Guide to Finding Your Way through Life's Ordeals* (New York: Gotham Books, 2004), 59–60.
3. Diane Ackerman, *A Natural History of the Senses* (New York: Random House, 1990), 277–78.
4. Moore, *Dark Nights of the Soul,* 59–60.

CHAPTER 5: EXPRESSION

1. Mary Pipher, *Writing to Change the World* (New York: Riverhead Books, 2006), 11.

2. Anne Lamott, *Bird by Bird: Some Instructions on Writing and Life* (New York: Anchor Books, 1995), 201.

CHAPTER 6: AWAKENING

1. Richard Carlson and Benjamin Shield, eds., *Handbook for the Soul* (Boston: Little, Brown, and Company, 1995).

2. Jaimal Yogis, "The Zen of Surfing," *Utne* (July–August 2006): 84–85.

CHAPTER 7: CELEBRATION

1. Neale Donald Walsch, *Communion with God* (New York: Putnam's Sons, 2000), 119–20.

2. Oriah Mountain Dreamer, *The Dance: Moving to the Rhythms of Your True Self* (New York: HarperCollins, 2001), 7–8.

CHAPTER 8: CONNECTION

1. Robert Benson, *Living Prayer* (New York: J. P. Tarcher, 1998), 27–28.

Acknowledgments

Many people have helped me coax this book into its present form. I am grateful to:

Maura Shaw. Without your faith and vision, this book would have remained in my heart. Thank you for calling on me for this great task!

Emily Wichland, Sarah McBride, Jenny Buono, and the staff of SkyLight Paths. Your follow-through and gentle persistence guided me through this process. Thank you for teaching me.

Marcia Broucek, my editor. You are a sculptor and a visionary. Thank you for gently and patiently polishing this stone.

The contributors. Your words and artwork inspire me in so many ways. I'm so honored to have a little piece of you in this book!

John, my husband. You got tears in your eyes the day we realized the idea of this book would become a reality, and you've continued to celebrate with me since. Thank you for your ceaseless support and enthusiasm ... and for helping me to think differently every day.

My family. You joyfully encouraged this project as the right step along my journey, just as you have encouraged every other endeavor. Thank you for your acceptance and confidence.

The readers of my manuscript, especially Melissa and Andre Javier-Barry, Jonathan Miller, Derek Easley, and Gary and Lynne Richardson. Your comments strengthened me and challenged me. Thank you for helping me to see through your eyes.

The 2005 Honorable Mentions. Your support and guidance were invaluable during this process, and your humor and creativity are a gift to me every day. Thank you for your loyalty and insight. Mostly, thank you for your presence.

And finally, the scrapbooking community. Thank you for creating a place of expression, learning, and support. Thank you for having the courage to share your stories and for inspiring others to do the same.

Children's Spiritual Biography

MULTICULTURAL, NONDENOMINATIONAL, NONSECTARIAN

Ten Amazing People
And How They Changed the World
by Maura D. Shaw; Foreword by Dr. Robert Coles
Full-color illus. by Stephen Marchesi

For ages
7 & up

Black Elk • Dorothy Day • Malcolm X • Mahatma Gandhi • Martin Luther King, Jr. • Mother Teresa • Janusz Korczak • Desmond Tutu • Thich Nhat Hanh • Albert Schweitzer

This vivid, inspirational and authoritative book will open new possibilities for children by telling the stories of how ten of the past century's greatest leaders changed the world in important ways.

8½ x 11, 48 pp, HC, Full-color illus., 978-1-893361-47-8 **$17.95**
For ages 7 & up

Spiritual Biographies for Young People—For ages 7 and up

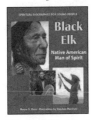
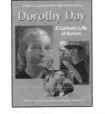
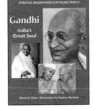
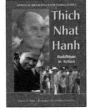

Black Elk: Native American Man of Spirit
by Maura D. Shaw; Full-color illus. by Stephen Marchesi
Through historically accurate illustrations and photos, inspiring age-appropriate activities and Black Elk's own words, this colorful biography introduces children to a remarkable person who ensured that the traditions and beliefs of his people would not be forgotten.
6¾ x 8¾, 32 pp, HC, Full-color and b/w illus., 978-1-59473-043-6 **$12.99**

Dorothy Day: A Catholic Life of Action
by Maura D. Shaw; Full-color illus. by Stephen Marchesi
Introduces children to one of the most inspiring women of the twentieth century, a down-to-earth spiritual leader who saw the presence of God in every person she met. Includes practical activities, a timeline and a list of important words to know.
6¾ x 8¾, 32 pp, HC, Full-color illus., 978-1-59473-011-5 **$12.99**

Gandhi: India's Great Soul
by Maura D. Shaw; Full-color illus. by Stephen Marchesi
There are a number of biographies of Gandhi written for young readers, but this is the only one that balances a simple text with illustrations, photographs, and activities that encourage children and adults to talk about how to make changes happen without violence. Introduces children to important concepts of freedom, equality and justice among people of all backgrounds and religions.
6¾ x 8¾, 32 pp, HC, Full-color illus., 978-1-893361-91-1 **$12.95**

Thich Nhat Hanh: Buddhism in Action
by Maura D. Shaw; Full-color illus. by Stephen Marchesi
Warm illustrations, photos, age-appropriate activities and Thich Nhat Hanh's own poems introduce a great man to children in a way they can understand and enjoy. Includes a list of important Buddhist words to know.
6¾ x 8¾, 32 pp, HC, Full-color illus., 978-1-893361-87-4 **$12.95**

Children's Spirituality—Board Books

Adam and Eve's New Day (A Board Book)
by Sandy Eisenberg Sasso; Full-color illus. by Joani Keller Rothenberg
A lesson in hope for every child who has worried about what comes next.
Abridged from *Adam and Eve's First Sunset.*
5 x 5, 24 pp, Full-color illus., Board Book, 978-1-59473-205-8 **$7.99** *For ages 0–4*

How Did the Animals Help God? (A Board Book)
by Nancy Sohn Swartz; Full-color illus. by Melanie Hall
Abridged from *In Our Image*, God asks all of nature to offer gifts to humankind—
with a promise that they will care for creation in return.
5 x 5, 24 pp, Board Book, Full-color illus., 978-1-59473-044-3 **$7.99** *For ages 0–4*

Where Is God? (A Board Book) by Lawrence and Karen Kushner; Full-color illus. by
Dawn W. Majewski A gentle way for young children to explore how God is with
us every day, in every way. Abridged from *Because Nothing Looks Like God.*
5 x 5, 24 pp, Board Book, Full-color illus., 978-1-893361-17-1 **$7.99** *For ages 0–4*

What Does God Look Like? (A Board Book)
by Lawrence and Karen Kushner; Full-color illus. by Dawn W. Majewski
A simple way for young children to explore the ways that we "see" God. Abridged
from *Because Nothing Looks Like God.*
5 x 5, 24 pp, Board Book, Full-color illus., 978-1-893361-23-2 **$7.95** *For ages 0–4*

How Does God Make Things Happen? (A Board Book)
by Lawrence and Karen Kushner; Full-color illus. by Dawn W. Majewski
A charming invitation for young children to explore how God makes things happen in
our world. Abridged from *Because Nothing Looks Like God.*
5 x 5, 24 pp, Board Book, Full-color illus., 978-1-893361-24-9 **$7.95** *For ages 0–4*

What Is God's Name? (A Board Book)
by Sandy Eisenberg Sasso; Full-color illus. by Phoebe Stone
Everyone and everything in the world has a name. What is God's name?
Abridged from the award-winning *In God's Name.*
5 x 5, 24 pp, Board Book, Full-color illus., 978-1-893361-10-2 **$7.99** *For ages 0–4*

What You Will See Inside ...

This important new series of books, each with many full-color photos, is
designed to show children ages 6 and up the Who, What, When, Where, Why
and How of traditional houses of worship, liturgical celebrations, and rituals of
different world faiths, empowering them to respect and understand their own
religious traditions—and those of their friends and neighbors.

What You Will See Inside a Catholic Church
by Reverend Michael Keane; Foreword by Robert J. Keeley, EdD
Full-color photos by Aaron Pepis
8½ x 10½, 32 pp, Full-color photos, HC, 978-1-893361-54-6 **$17.95**

Also available in Spanish: **Lo que se puede ver dentro de una iglesia católica**
8½ x 10½, 32 pp, Full-color photos, HC, 978-1-893361-66-9 **$16.95**

What You Will See Inside a Hindu Temple
by Dr. Mahendra Jani and Dr. Vandana Jani; Full-color photos by Neirah Bhargava and Vijay Dave
8½ x 10½, 32 pp, Full-color photos, HC, 978-1-59473-116-7 **$17.99**

What You Will See Inside a Mosque
by Aisha Karen Khan; Full-color photos by Aaron Pepis
8½ x 10½, 32 pp, Full-color photos, HC, 978-1-893361-60-7 **$16.95**

What You Will See Inside a Synagogue
by Rabbi Lawrence A. Hoffman and Dr. Ron Wolfson; Full-color photos by Bill Aron
8½ x 10½, 32 pp, Full-color photos, HC, 978-1-59473-012-2 **$17.99**

Children's Spirituality

Adam and Eve's First Sunset: God's New Day
by Sandy Eisenberg Sasso; Full-color illus. by Joani Keller Rothenberg
9 x 12, 32 pp, Full-color illus., HC, 978-1-58023-177-0 **$17.95** *For ages 4 & up (a Jewish Lights book)*

Because Nothing Looks Like God
by Lawrence and Karen Kushner; Full-color illus. by Dawn W. Majewski
Real-life examples of happiness and sadness introduce children to the possibilities of spiritual life. 11 x 8½, 32 pp, HC, Full-color illus., 978-1-58023-092-6 **$16.95**
For ages 4 & up (a Jewish Lights book)

Also available: **Teacher's Guide,** 8½ x 11, 22 pp, PB, 978-1-58023-140-4 **$6.95** *For ages 5–8*

Becoming Me: A Story of Creation
by Martin Boroson; Full-color illus. by Christopher Gilvan-Cartwright
Told in the personal "voice" of the Creator, a story about creation and relationship that is about each one of us.
8 x 10, 32 pp, Full-color illus., HC, 978-1-893361-11-9 **$16.95** *For ages 4 & up*

But God Remembered: Stories of Women from Creation to the
Promised Land   *by Sandy Eisenberg Sasso; Full-color illus. by Bethanne Andersen*
A fascinating collection of four different stories of women only briefly mentioned in biblical tradition and religious texts. 9 x 12, 32 pp, HC, Full-color illus., 978-1-879045-43-9 **$16.95**
For ages 8 & up (a Jewish Lights book)

Cain & Abel: Finding the Fruits of Peace
by Sandy Eisenberg Sasso; Full-color illus. by Joani Keller Rothenberg
A sensitive recasting of the ancient tale shows we have the power to deal with anger in positive ways. "Editor's Choice"—American Library Association's *Booklist*
9 x 12, 32 pp, HC, Full-color illus., 978-1-58023-123-7 **$16.95** *For ages 5 & up (a Jewish Lights book)*

Does God Hear My Prayer?
by August Gold; Full-color photos by Diane Hardy Waller
Introduces preschoolers and young readers to prayer and how it helps them express their own emotions. 10 x 8½, 32 pp, Quality PB, Full-color photo illus., 978-1-59473-102-0 **$8.99**

The 11th Commandment: Wisdom from Our Children *by The Children of America*
"If there were an Eleventh Commandment, what would it be?" Children of many religious denominations across America answer this question—in their own drawings and words. "A rare book of spiritual celebration for all people, of all ages, for all time." —*Bookviews*
8 x 10, 48 pp, HC, Full-color illus., 978-1-879045-46-0 **$16.95** *For all ages (a Jewish Lights book)*

For Heaven's Sake *by Sandy Eisenberg Sasso; Full-color illus. by Kathryn Kunz Finney*
Everyone talked about heaven: "Thank heavens." "Heaven forbid." "For heaven's sake, Isaiah." But no one would say what heaven was or how to find it. So Isaiah decides to find out, by seeking answers from many different people.
9 x 12, 32 pp, HC, Full-color illus., 978-1-58023-054-4 **$16.95** *For ages 4 & up (a Jewish Lights book)*

God in Between *by Sandy Eisenberg Sasso; Full-color illus. by Sally Sweetland*
A magical, mythical tale that teaches that God can be found where we are.
9 x 12, 32 pp, HC, Full-color illus., 978-1-879045-86-6 **$16.95** *For ages 4 & up (a Jewish Lights book)*

God's Paintbrush: Special 10th Anniversary Edition
Invites children of all faiths and backgrounds to encounter God through moments in their own lives. 11 x 8½, 32 pp, Full-color illus., HC, 978-1-58023-195-4 **$17.95** *For ages 4 & up*

Also available: **God's Paintbrush Teacher's Guide** 8½ x 11, 32 pp, PB, 978-1-879045-57-6 **$8.95**

God's Paintbrush Celebration Kit
A Spiritual Activity Kit for Teachers and Students of All Faiths, All Backgrounds
Additional activity sheets available:
8-Student Activity Sheet Pack (40 sheets/5 sessions), 978-1-58023-058-2 **$19.95**
Single-Student Activity Sheet Pack (5 sessions), 978-1-58023-059-9 **$3.95**

Meditation / Prayer

Prayers to an Evolutionary God
by William Cleary; Afterword by Diarmuid O'Murchu
How is it possible to pray when God is dislocated from heaven, dispersed all around us, and more of a creative force than an all-knowing father? Inspired by the spiritual and scientific teachings of Diarmuid O'Murchu and Teilhard de Chardin, Cleary reveals that religion and science can be combined to create an expanding view of the universe—an evolutionary faith.
6 x 9, 208 pp, HC, 978-1-59473-006-1 **$21.99**

Psalms: A Spiritual Commentary
by M. Basil Pennington, ocso; Illustrations by Phillip Ratner
Showing how the Psalms give profound and candid expression to both our highest aspirations and our deepest pain, the late, highly respected Cistercian Abbot M. Basil Pennington shares his reflections on some of the most beloved passages from the Bible's most widely read book.
6 x 9, 176 pp, HC, 24 full-page b/w illus., 978-1-59473-141-9 **$19.99**

The Song of Songs: A Spiritual Commentary
by M. Basil Pennington, ocso; Illustrations by Phillip Ratner
Join the late M. Basil Pennington as he ruminates on the Bible's most challenging mystical text. Follow a path into the Songs that weaves through his inspired words and the evocative drawings of Jewish artist Phillip Ratner—a path that reveals your own humanity and leads to the deepest delight of your soul.
6 x 9, 160 pp, HC, 14 b/w illus., 978-1-59473-004-7 **$19.99**

Women of Color Pray: Voices of Strength, Faith, Healing, Hope and Courage *Edited and with Introductions by Christal M. Jackson*
Through these prayers, poetry, lyrics, meditations and affirmations, you will share in the strong and undeniable connection women of color share with God. It will challenge you to explore new ways of prayerful expression.
5 x 7¼, 208 pp, Quality PB, 978-1-59473-077-1 **$15.99**

The Art of Public Prayer: Not for Clergy Only
by Lawrence A. Hoffman
An ecumenical resource for all people looking to change hardened worship patterns.
6 x 9, 288 pp, Quality PB, 978-1-893361-06-5 **$18.99**

Finding Grace at the Center, 3rd Ed.: The Beginning of Centering Prayer
by M. Basil Pennington, ocso, Thomas Keating, ocso, and Thomas E. Clarke, sj Foreword by Rev. Cynthia Bourgeault, PhD
5 x 7¼, 128 pp, Quality PB, 978-1-59473-182-2 **$12.99**

A Heart of Stillness: A Complete Guide to Learning the Art of Meditation
by David A. Cooper 5½ x 8½, 272 pp, Quality PB, 978-1-893361-03-4 **$16.95**

Meditation without Gurus: A Guide to the Heart of Practice
by Clark Strand 5½ x 8½, 192 pp, Quality PB, 978-1-893361-93-5 **$16.95**

Praying with Our Hands: 21 Practices of Embodied Prayer from the World's Spiritual Traditions *by Jon M. Sweeney; Photographs by Jennifer J. Wilson; Foreword by Mother Tessa Bielecki; Afterword by Taitetsu Unno, PhD*
8 x 8, 96 pp, 22 duotone photos, Quality PB, 978-1-893361-16-4 **$16.95**

Silence, Simplicity & Solitude: A Complete Guide to Spiritual Retreat at Home
by David A. Cooper 5½ x 8½, 336 pp, Quality PB, 978-1-893361-04-1 **$16.95**

Three Gates to Meditation Practice: A Personal Journey into Sufism, Buddhism, and Judaism *by David A. Cooper* 5½ x 8½, 240 pp, Quality PB, 978-1-893361-22-5 **$16.95**

Women Pray: Voices through the Ages, from Many Faiths, Cultures and Traditions
Edited and with Introductions by Monica Furlong
5 x 7¼, 256 pp, Quality PB, 978-1-59473-071-9 **$15.99**
Deluxe HC with ribbon marker, 978-1-893361-25-6 **$19.95**

Spirituality of the Seasons

Autumn: A Spiritual Biography of the Season
Edited by Gary Schmidt and Susan M. Felch; Illustrations by Mary Azarian
Rejoice in autumn as a time of preparation and reflection. Includes Wendell Berry, David James Duncan, Robert Frost, A. Bartlett Giamatti, E. B. White, P. D. James, Julian of Norwich, Garret Keizer, Tracy Kidder, Anne Lamott, May Sarton.
6 x 9, 320 pp, 5 b/w illus., Quality PB, 978-1-59473-118-1 **$18.99**
HC, 978-1-59473-005-4 **$22.99**

Spring: A Spiritual Biography of the Season
Edited by Gary Schmidt and Susan M. Felch; Illustrations by Mary Azarian
Explore the gentle unfurling of spring and reflect on how nature celebrates rebirth and renewal. Includes Jane Kenyon, Lucy Larcom, Harry Thurston, Nathaniel Hawthorne, Noel Perrin, Annie Dillard, Martha Ballard, Barbara Kingsolver, Dorothy Wordsworth, Donald Hall, David Brill, Lionel Basney, Isak Dinesen, Paul Laurence Dunbar.
6 x 9, 352 pp, 6 b/w illus., HC, 978-1-59473-114-3 **$21.99**

Summer: A Spiritual Biography of the Season
Edited by Gary Schmidt and Susan M. Felch; Illustrations by Barry Moser
"A sumptuous banquet.... These selections lift up an exquisite wholeness found within an everyday sophistication."— ★ *Publishers Weekly* starred review
Includes Anne Lamott, Luci Shaw, Ray Bradbury, Richard Selzer, Thomas Lynch, Walt Whitman, Carl Sandburg, Sherman Alexie, Madeleine L'Engle, Jamaica Kincaid.
6 x 9, 304 pp, 5 b/w illus., HC, 978-1-59473-083-2 **$21.99**

Winter: A Spiritual Biography of the Season
Edited by Gary Schmidt and Susan M. Felch; Illustrations by Barry Moser
"This outstanding anthology features top-flight nature and spirituality writers on the fierce, inexorable season of winter.... Remarkably lively and warm, despite the icy subject." — ★ *Publishers Weekly* starred review.
Includes Will Campbell, Rachel Carson, Annie Dillard, Donald Hall, Ron Hansen, Jane Kenyon, Jamaica Kincaid, Barry Lopez, Kathleen Norris, John Updike, E. B. White.
6 x 9, 288 pp, 6 b/w illus., Deluxe PB w/flaps, 978-1-893361-92-8 **$18.95**
HC, 978-1-893361-53-9 **$21.95**

Spirituality / Animal Companions

Blessing the Animals: Prayers and Ceremonies to Celebrate God's Creatures, Wild and Tame *Edited by Lynn L. Caruso* 5 x 7¼, 256 pp, HC, 978-1-59473-145-7 **$19.99**

What Animals Can Teach Us about Spirituality: Inspiring Lessons from Wild and Tame Creatures *by Diana L. Guerrero* 6 x 9, 176 pp, Quality PB, 978-1-893361-84-3 **$16.95**

Spirituality

Awakening the Spirit, Inspiring the Soul
30 Stories of Interspiritual Discovery in the Community of Faiths
Edited by Brother Wayne Teasdale and Martha Howard, MD; Foreword by Joan Borysenko, PhD
Thirty original spiritual mini-autobiographies showcase the varied ways that people come to faith—and what that means—in today's multi-religious world.
6 x 9, 224 pp, HC, 978-1-59473-039-9 **$21.99**

The Alphabet of Paradise: An A–Z of Spirituality for Everyday Life
by Howard Cooper 5 x 7¼, 224 pp, Quality PB, 978-1-893361-80-5 **$16.95**

Creating a Spiritual Retirement: A Guide to the Unseen Possibilities in Our Lives
by Molly Srode 6 x 9, 208 pp, b/w photos, Quality PB, 978-1-59473-050-4 **$14.99**
HC, 978-1-893361-75-1 **$19.95**

Finding Hope: Cultivating God's Gift of a Hopeful Spirit
by Marcia Ford 8 x 8, 200 pp, Quality PB, 978-1-59473-211-9 **$16.99**

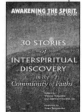

The Geography of Faith: Underground Conversations on Religious, Political and Social Change *by Daniel Berrigan and Robert Coles* 6 x 9, 224 pp, Quality PB, 978-1-893361-40-9 **$16.95**

God Within: Our Spiritual Future—As Told by Today's New Adults *Edited by Jon M. Sweeney and the Editors at SkyLight Paths* 6 x 9, 176 pp, Quality PB, 978-1-893361-15-7 **$14.95**

Spirituality

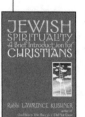

Jewish Spirituality: A Brief Introduction for Christians *by Lawrence Kushner*
5½ x 8½, 112 pp, Quality PB, 978-1-58023-150-3 **$12.95** *(a Jewish Lights book)*

Journeys of Simplicity: Traveling Light with Thomas Merton, Bashō, Edward Abbey,
Annie Dillard & Others *by Philip Harnden* 5 x 7¼, 128 pp, HC, 978-1-893361-76-8 **$16.95**

Keeping Spiritual Balance As We Grow Older: More than 65 Creative Ways to
Use Purpose, Prayer, and the Power of Spirit to Build a Meaningful Retirement
by Molly and Bernie Srode 8 x 8, 224 pp, Quality PB, 978-1-59473-042-9 **$16.99**

The Monks of Mount Athos: A Western Monk's Extraordinary Spiritual Journey on
Eastern Holy Ground *by M. Basil Pennington, ocso; Foreword by Archimandrite Dionysios*
6 x 9, 256 pp, 10+ b/w line drawings, Quality PB, 978-1-893361-78-2 **$18.95**

One God Clapping: The Spiritual Path of a Zen Rabbi *by Alan Lew with Sherrill Jaffe*
5½ x 8½, 336 pp, Quality PB, 978-1-58023-115-2 **$16.95** *(a Jewish Lights book)*

Prayer for People Who Think Too Much: A Guide to Everyday, Anywhere Prayer
from the World's Faith Traditions *by Mitch Finley*
5½ x 8½, 224 pp, Quality PB, 978-1-893361-21-8 **$16.99**; HC, 978-1-893361-00-3 **$21.95**

Show Me Your Way: The Complete Guide to Exploring Interfaith Spiritual Direction
by Howard A. Addison 5½ x 8½, 240 pp, Quality PB, 978-1-893361-41-6 **$16.95**

Spirituality 101: The Indispensable Guide to Keeping—or Finding—Your Spiritual Life
on Campus *by Harriet L. Schwartz, with contributions from college students at nearly thirty
campuses across the United States* 6 x 9, 272 pp, Quality PB, 978-1-59473-000-9 **$16.99**

Spiritually Incorrect: Finding God in All the *Wrong* Places *by Dan Wakefield; Illus. by
Marian DelVecchio* 5½ x 8½, 192 pp, b/w illus., Quality PB, 978-1-59473-137-2 **$15.99**

Spiritual Manifestos: Visions for Renewed Religious Life in America from Young
Spiritual Leaders of Many Faiths *Edited by Niles Elliot Goldstein; Preface by Martin E. Marty*
6 x 9, 256 pp, HC, 978-1-893361-09-6 **$21.95**

A Walk with Four Spiritual Guides: Krishna, Buddha, Jesus, and Ramakrishna
by Andrew Harvey 5½ x 8½, 192 pp, 10 b/w photos & illus.,Quality PB, 978-1-59473-138-9 **$15.99**

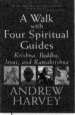

What Matters: Spiritual Nourishment for Head and Heart
by Frederick Franck 5 x 7¼, 128 pp, 50+ b/w illus., HC, 978-1-59473-013-9 **$16.99**

Who Is My God?, 2nd Edition: An Innovative Guide to Finding Your Spiritual Identity
Created by the Editors at SkyLight Paths 6 x 9, 160 pp, Quality PB, 978-1-59473-014-6 **$15.99**

Spirituality—A Week Inside

Come and Sit: A Week Inside Meditation Centers
by Marcia Z. Nelson; Foreword by Wayne Teasdale
The insider's guide to meditation in a variety of different spiritual traditions—
Buddhist, Hindu, Christian, Jewish, and Sufi traditions.
6 x 9, 224 pp, b/w photos, Quality PB, 978-1-893361-35-5 **$16.95**

Lighting the Lamp of Wisdom: A Week Inside a Yoga Ashram
by John Ittner; Foreword by Dr. David Frawley
This insider's guide to Hindu spiritual life takes you into a typical week of retreat
inside a yoga ashram to demystify the experience and show you what to expect.
6 x 9, 192 pp, 10+ b/w photos, Quality PB, 978-1-893361-52-2 **$15.95**

Making a Heart for God: A Week Inside a Catholic Monastery
by Dianne Aprile; Foreword by Brother Patrick Hart, ocso
Takes you to the Abbey of Gethsemani—the Trappist monastery in Kentucky
that was home to author Thomas Merton—to explore the details.
6 x 9, 224 pp, b/w photos, Quality PB, 978-1-893361-49-2 **$16.95**

Waking Up: A Week Inside a Zen Monastery
by Jack Maguire; Foreword by John Daido Loori, Roshi
An essential guide to what it's like to spend a week inside a Zen Buddhist monastery.
6 x 9, 224 pp, b/w photos, Quality PB, 978-1-893361-55-3 **$16.95**
HC, 978-1-893361-13-3 **$21.95**

Spirituality & Crafts

The Knitting Way: A Guide to Spiritual Self-Discovery
by Linda Skolnik and Janice MacDaniels
7 x 9, 240 pp, Quality PB, 978-1-59473-079-5 **$16.99**

The Quilting Path
A Guide to Spiritual Discovery through Fabric, Thread and Kabbalah
by Louise Silk
7 x 9, 192 pp, Quality PB, 978-1-59473-206-5 **$16.99**

Spiritual Practice

Divining the Body
Reclaim the Holiness of Your Physical Self *by Jan Phillips*
A practical and inspiring guidebook for connecting the body and soul in spiritual practice. Leads you into a milieu of reverence, mystery and delight, helping you discover your body as a pathway to the Divine.
8 x 8, 256 pp, Quality PB, 978-1-59473-080-1 **$16.99**

Finding Time for the Timeless: Spirituality in the Workweek
by John McQuiston II
Simple, refreshing stories that provide you with examples of how you can refocus and enrich your daily life using prayer or meditation, ritual and other forms of spiritual practice. 5½ x 6¾, 208 pp, HC, 978-1-59473-035-1 **$17.99**

The Gospel of Thomas
A Guidebook for Spiritual Practice *by Ron Miller; Translations by Stevan Davies*
An innovative guide to bring a new spiritual classic into daily life.
6 x 9, 160 pp, Quality PB, 978-1-59473-047-4 **$14.99**

Earth, Water, Fire, and Air: Essential Ways of Connecting to Spirit
by Cait Johnson 6 x 9, 224 pp, HC, 978-1-893361-65-2 **$19.95**

Labyrinths from the Outside In: Walking to Spiritual Insight—A Beginner's Guide
by Donna Schaper and Carole Ann Camp
6 x 9, 208 pp, b/w illus. and photos, Quality PB, 978-1-893361-18-8 **$16.95**

Practicing the Sacred Art of Listening: A Guide to Enrich Your Relationships and Kindle Your Spiritual Life—The Listening Center Workshop
by Kay Lindahl 8 x 8, 176 pp, Quality PB, 978-1-893361-85-0 **$16.95**

Releasing the Creative Spirit: Unleash the Creativity in Your Life
by Dan Wakefield 7 x 10, 256 pp, Quality PB, 978-1-893361-36-2 **$16.95**

The Sacred Art of Bowing: Preparing to Practice
by Andi Young 5½ x 8½, 128 pp, b/w illus., Quality PB, 978-1-893361-82-9 **$14.95**

The Sacred Art of Chant: Preparing to Practice
by Ana Hernández 5½ x 8½, 192 pp, Quality PB, 978-1-59473-036-8 **$15.99**

The Sacred Art of Fasting: Preparing to Practice
by Thomas Ryan, CSP 5½ x 8½, 192 pp, Quality PB, 978-1-59473-078-8 **$15.99**

The Sacred Art of Forgiveness: Forgiving Ourselves and Others through God's Grace
by Marcia Ford 8 x 8, 176 pp, Quality PB, 978-1-59473-175-4 **$16.99**

The Sacred Art of Listening: Forty Reflections for Cultivating a Spiritual Practice
by Kay Lindahl; Illustrations by Amy Schnapper
8 x 8, 160 pp, b/w illus., Quality PB, 978-1-893361-44-7 **$16.99**

The Sacred Art of Lovingkindness: Preparing to Practice
by Rabbi Rami Shapiro; Foreword by Marcia Ford
5½ x 8½, 176 pp, Quality PB, 978-1-59473-151-8 **$16.99**

Sacred Speech: A Practical Guide for Keeping Spirit in Your Speech
by Rev. Donna Schaper 6 x 9, 176 pp, Quality PB, 978-1-59473-068-9 **$15.99**
HC, 978-1-893361-74-4 **$21.95**

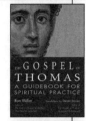

About SKYLIGHT PATHS Publishing

SkyLight Paths Publishing is creating a place where people of different spiritual traditions come together for challenge and inspiration, a place where we can help each other understand the mystery that lies at the heart of our existence.

Through spirituality, our religious beliefs are increasingly becoming a part of our lives—rather than *apart* from our lives. While many of us may be more interested than ever in spiritual growth, we may be less firmly planted in traditional religion. Yet, we do want to deepen our relationship to the sacred, to learn from our own as well as from other faith traditions, and to practice in new ways.

SkyLight Paths sees both believers and seekers as a community that increasingly transcends traditional boundaries of religion and denomination—people wanting to learn from each other, *walking together, finding the way.*

For your information and convenience, at the back of this book we have provided a list of other SkyLight Paths books you might find interesting and useful. They cover the following subjects:

Buddhism / Zen	Gnosticism	Mysticism
Catholicism	Hinduism /	Poetry
Children's Books	Vedanta	Prayer
Christianity	Inspiration	Religious Etiquette
Comparative	Islam / Sufism	Retirement
Religion	Judaism / Kabbalah /	Spiritual Biography
Current Events	Enneagram	Spiritual Direction
Earth-Based	Meditation	Spirituality
Spirituality	Midrash Fiction	Women's Interest
Global Spiritual	Monasticism	Worship
Perspectives		

Or phone, fax, mail or e-mail to: SKYLIGHT PATHS Publishing
Sunset Farm Offices, Route 4 • P.O. Box 237 • Woodstock, Vermont 05091
Tel: (802) 457-4000 • Fax: (802) 457-4004 • www.skylightpaths.com
Credit card orders: (800) 962-4544 (8:30AM–5:30PM ET Monday–Friday)
Generous discounts on quantity orders. SATISFACTION GUARANTEED. Prices subject to change.